LAW AND ORDER IN GRADE 6-E

LAW AND ORDER IN GRADE 6-E

A Story of Chaos and Innovation in a Ghetto School

by Kim Marshall

with Photographs by the Author

Little, Brown and Company   Boston   Toronto

Portions of this book originally appeared in somewhat different form in the *Harvard Bulletin*.

Library of Congress Cataloging in Publication Data

Marshall, Kim.
    Law and order in Grade Six-E.

    1. Martin Luther King Middle School. 2. Educational
innovations--U. S. 3. Education, Urban--Boston.
I. Title.
LB1027.M319   371.3   72-1814
ISBN 0-316-54690-9

Published simultaneously in Canada by Little, Brown & Company (Canada) Limited

Printed in the United States of America

This book is dedicated to my students of the past three years, and to their futures.

Grade 6-E: Deborah, Peter, Sharnitha, Angela, Michael, Debra, Lawrence, Randy, David, Elizabeth, John, Valerie, Sheila, Clarence, Willie, Elaine, Richard, Job, Marilyn, Melody, Gloria, James, Yvonne, Robert, Louise, Lillian, Phyllis, Clifford, Judy, Esau, Brenda and Jimmy.

Grade 6-G: Edwin, Leroy, John C., Cynthia S., Martheina, Celia, Charlie, Bonita, Jerome, Reginald, Barbara, Cassandra, Cynthia G., Michael, Starr, Joyce, Norris, Sarah, Elsa, Dianne, Ingrid, Linda, Kim, John P., Theodus, Lorraine, Alvaro, and Ethel.

Grade 6-D: Alphonso, Douglas, Vickey, Lynn, Lolethia, Donald, John, Thomas, Juey, Joseph, Delores, Patricia, Steven, Kassedra, Yvonne, Almaria, Rennell, Johnny, Louis, Ulysses, Eric, Trina, Charles, Gina, James, and Cornelius.

Acknowledgments

I would like to thank John Bethel, editor of the Harvard *Bulletin,* for his encouragement and superb editing of the two magazine articles which led up to this book; Ivar Viehe-Naess for making final prints of my photographs; and a number of people who helped with drafts of the two *Bulletin* articles and the manuscript of this book: Rudd Crawford, Peter Thon, Dick Mc-Adoo, Mike and Betsy Useem, Peter and Kathy Rousmaniere, Craig Coggins, Peter DeStefano, Jim Howard, and Rosina Coolidge. I am especially grateful to Dick McAdoo, whose suggestion it was to make the two articles into a book, and whose comments and criticisms made them into a book.

I am also grateful for the support and encouragement of the two principals under whom I have taught, Rollins Griffith and Will Ella Brown, and to the ideas, inspiration, criticism, and help given me by many others, among them: Warren Chafe, Wilton Anderson, Brad Crawford, Paul and Maureen Casilli, John Dempsey, David Mirsky, Marty McCahill, Myles Striar, Edward Banfield, John Holden, Corb and Laurie Smith, Ellen Meisels, Bill and Carol Schneider, Dolores Jackson, Ruth Andrews, and my family.

I also owe a tremendous amount to my students — they have taught me most of what I know about teaching. I have used pseudonyms in the text, but their real names appear in the Dedication and most of the members of Grade 6-G have their pictures spread through the book and on the back cover.

And most especially I am grateful to Rhoda.

Contents

LAW AND ORDER
IN GRADE 6-E

One.

The King School

In the summer of 1969, right after I graduated from college, I got a job teaching sixth grade at the Martin Luther King Middle School in Boston. I was hired by a young black man who had just been appointed principal of the all-black school that August; when I began teaching Grade 6-E in early September, I found that he was responsible for something of a turning point in the school's tumultuous history.

The King School is the public school for the sixth, seventh, and eighth grades in Grove Hall, a tough area of Boston's mainly black Roxbury. The school is within the Boston Model Cities Area and is just a few blocks to the east of Washington Park, which has been dramatically cleaned up and rehabilitated with federal money over the last few years. But although there is an unusually large number of political, social, and religious groups active in Grove Hall, it is a slum. The bombed-out appearance of "the strip" of Blue Hill Avenue down the hill from the King School has become notorious in Boston, the subject of several newspaper features bewailing the effects of the 1967 riot in the area and the flight of the white middle class and small businesses to the suburbs. The amount of violent (often drug-related) crime in the area spurred the formation of one of the nation's first all-black police contingents in November of 1971, but the Soul Patrol" has a tough job ahead of it with the number of drug addicts, drunks, pimps and prostitutes who haunt the streets and abandoned houses, enticing the community's young people. Unemployment in Roxbury is around twenty percent, and is even higher for teen-agers and young men, and the social emasculation of many black men has expressed itself in a large number of broken homes and heavy burdens on the mothers and grandmothers and sisters who remain to take care of those homes. While Grove Hall does not have the open gang warfare of Philadelphia's ghetto, where a boy can be killed for stepping outside his "territory," or the level of heroin addiction of Harlem, where grade school children have died of overdoses, this area is rife with all the social and personal problems of a ghetto and is rapidly worsening.

It has not always been this way, as many of the Jews and Irish Catholics who lived in the same neighborhood in previous decades will tell you. The last ten years have seen a dramatic shift from a white ethnic to an almost completely black and Puerto Rican population. The King School, which was called the Patrick T. Campbell School before 1968, reacted to this new environment like someone waking up in a strange place. The mostly white staff found the community an increasingly hostile environment and moved to other parts of the city or the suburbs, driving to the school every day. Methods of teaching and handling kids that had apparently worked before were suddenly met with stubborn and sometimes explosive resistance by the new generation of black students. Inexorably the number of fights, false fire alarms, "uncontrolled" classes, assaults on teachers, and cases of arson inside the school rose. Inevitably many of the former teachers and administrators of the school left, saying that they could not understand or deal with the behavior of the students.

Indeed, growing up in Grove Hall today is an experience that is alien to the childhood memories of most teachers. I am convinced that I would not have survived an early adolescence of so many fights, predatory bullies, shakedowns, and stolen bicycles, of such great pressure to get involved in promiscuous sex, car theft, vandalism and drugs. These experiences give the kids who do survive a veneer of cool and impenetrable toughness at an early age.

Besides their differences in experiences from the new

black students, teachers in the Campbell School in this transitional period were often put in the position of suppressing their students' energy and fighting their toughness. In the atmosphere of tension and increasing confusion, there seemed to be few opportunities for real communication between teachers and students, and in its absence the racial issue — black students versus white teachers and administrators — fed upon itself and further undermined the effectiveness of traditional authoritarian teaching.

Because the school provided few outlets for energy (no outdoor recess, no athletic program, an inadequate gym), because few staff members truly understood the problems of the community or communicated with the kids, and because few classes or other school activities were on the same wavelength as most of the students, the school did little to deal with the problems which its students brought into school with them. Instead it became a crucible of those problems, a place where they became more intense and more violent than they were in the outside community.

Mounting chaos in the Campbell School (and in other schools in Roxbury and North Dorchester) distressed many parents and others in the community. After a few scrapes with the Boston School Committee, many people came to feel that the public schools in the area were a lost cause, and tried to create alternatives. By 1971, two busing programs (one to other parts of Boston, one to the suburbs) and several community schools were taking about 2,300 black students (nine percent of the area's black school population) out of the Roxbury public schools. And in 1965 pressure from black and white liberal groups resulted in the passage of the Massachusetts Racial Imbalance Act, which was supposed to reduce the number of schools with more than fifty percent non-white students by the leverage of state funding.

But by 1968 the mood had changed. The Racial Imbalance Act proved almost totally ineffective, with racial polarization in the Boston schools increasing in the years after its passage. And the busing and independent school movements reached limits of tolerance and funding which prevented either from posing a competitive challenge to the Boston School Committee to improve the quality of Roxbury schools. More and more the emphasis in the black community shifted from integration and community schools to improving the quality of public schools in the community. Initially people hoped to improve the schools by making them more sympathetic to the community, and they began to press for black administrators and more black teachers. Some pressed for community control.

It was symbolic of this shift of mood that parents and community groups demanded that the Campbell School be renamed after Martin Luther King following his assassination in 1968. The Boston School Committee acquiesced, and the black community went on to press its demands for black administrators and staff. Soon afterward, the principal of the King School resigned, and the community seized the opportunity to mount a campaign for a black principal.

For the entire summer the school committee stubbornly refused to consider the idea of appointing a black man who was not on the rated list (there were none on the list at that time). But at the last moment the threat of violence and the possibility of a community take-over of the school convinced the school committee to appoint an elderly and very conservative black man as principal of the school. The timing of the concession outmaneuvered those who disapproved of the choice. It also allowed the school committee to say, "We told you a black principal was not the answer," when the new principal resigned that November, an exhausted and bitter man, in the midst of the worst violence the school had ever experienced.

The remainder of the year saw more abortive attempts to change the situation in the school. A three-day conference of parents, teachers, and local school officials in November worked out a series of proposals which might have had some effect. But the Boston School Committee felt threatened by the rhetoric of community control and by the involvement of some militants in the conference, and prevented the major ideas from being implemented. When a white principal was appointed to replace the black principal who had resigned, violence reached a crescendo and the school had to be closed for nearly two months while various groups tried to think of solutions.

The school reopened in February with a reduced enrollment and a number of ideas proposed by a group of teachers being tried out; but the success of the innovations was vitiated by an influx of students who had temporarily transferred away to other schools, and confusion returned. When school finally closed for the summer, three grades of students had received virtually no education during the year, having missed sixty-two days of school, and there was great bitterness in the community that so much activity around the school had not produced any results. Even more irksome was the fact that a three-year, $1,500,000 federal grant to promote innovation and community participation in the King School and a nearby junior high school had gone through its first year without being able to bring about any real changes — it set up a school-community advisory council, hired community aides (who spent most of their time guarding fire alarm boxes and patrolling the corridors), and bought movable furniture for most of the classrooms.

During the summer of 1969, various community groups badgered the school department to appoint a young black man as principal of the school. In August, to everyone's surprise, the department did. A thirty-five-year-old project director of an innovative junior high school in Roxbury was transferred to the King School and given wide powers to select his staff. (The fact that the new principal was not on the school department's rated list for appointing principals was considered by some a significant breakthrough.) During the summer, the new principal took advantage of his mandate from the school department and put together a staff almost one-third black, a remarkable accomplishment in Boston where blacks then comprised only five percent of the teaching force. He also convinced the authorities to "overstaff" the school, so that the student-teacher ratio in my first year of teaching was almost ten to one. During two weeks of staff workshops (which were also funded by the city) at the end of the summer there was a good deal of optimism in the staff about the year ahead.

To some degree the optimism was justified. For the entire school year the school was relatively stable. There were no false fire alarms. The corridors were quiet. Very few outsiders penetrated the tight security. The school seemed a going proposition for the first time in perhaps six years, and the community expressed its confidence in the principal by sending its children back to the school in large numbers; the enrollment climbed rapidly to around 650 students. The federally-funded advisory council was able to put fifteen community paraprofessionals to work in classrooms, furnish a first-rate library, buy lockers and copying equipment, and finance frequent visits by a group from the suburbs that did excellent science demonstrations. The advisory council also established some rapport with the school department and brought some specialists and equipment into the school. Later in the year the school department financed the construction of special Reading and Guidance areas and a paid hour after school for the entire staff for meetings and tutoring.

But there were still tensions in the King School. If anything, the problems had simply been squeezed from the corridors into the classrooms by the toughness, blackness, and vigor of the new administration. While the black principal and black teachers effectively neutralized the racial aspect of disruption, making it difficult to attack the school as a white racist institution, the job of teaching in individual classrooms remained a tremendous personal and professional challenge. Two of the three grades of students in the school had never thought of the King School as a quiet, productive, or friendly place, and many of the kids persisted in showing a certain amount of disrespect for teachers and administrators, both black and white.

In some classrooms good teaching, both traditional and innovative, began to take hold and change the attitudes of some kids. Communication between parents and the school was vastly improved, as was the community's confidence in the school. This combined with the tight discipline around the school to lay the foundations of what might become a deeper stability in the future.

This, then, was the history of the school and the general situation during the 1969-70 year, my first year of teaching with Grade 6-E. For reasons that will become obvious, my classroom was contributing very little in the way of discipline *or* innovation; in fact it was one of the most chaotic places in the school.

Two.

Law and Order in Grade 6-E

I came into my first year of teaching with a bachelor's degree in Government, a lot of general knowledge about the "urban crisis," ten credits in education courses taken over the summer, six weeks of practice teaching in a suburban summer school, a summer's work doing research for a report on the Boston public schools, some familiarity with the problems and some of the personalities of the King School from writing a long paper in college, and piles of good intentions. In short, I was *totally* unprepared to teach in the school. As the year progressed, I found this out and learned that being sincere and a nice guy was, if anything, a liability if you were without the skills to teach from day to day. I found that none of the "teacher books" I had read dealt at all honestly with the first-year trauma, but that within the school the thrashings and wailings of beginners was an old story. All the books had made it seem so easy, and I put them away and returned to reality with some bitterness.

The year began with high hopes and a proposed speech that would have taken forty-five minutes to deliver to my open-mouthed class. The prepared text made a number of points: we would not be afraid of asking questions on any subject, and there was to be a special signal that shy members of the class could flash if they didn't understand something; I should be seen as a source of solace and sympathy and students could come to me with all manner of problems; the desks would be arranged amphitheater-style for a more democratic atmosphere; students would work in groups and help each other on their work as soon as we got settled down; disorder would not be tolerated, but talking to teach each other would be fine; I would be in close touch with parents; and students should see themselves as part of a uniquely challenged group, the American blacks of the seventies.

Although I did arrange the desks around myself in a sort of amphitheater, I never gave the speech. For one thing, I got stage fright as my students filed in one by one and stared curiously and quietly at me; for another, I realized how meaningless so many empty resolutions were. Like the Nixon Administration, I decided to adopt the maxim, "Watch what we do, not what we say," and hoped I could deliver in the form of concrete actions that would speak for themselves. But like the Administration, my performance was nothing to get very excited about: I never delivered on some of my promises, delivered very late on others, and delivered in a half-assed manner on still others. Constraints that I hadn't dreamed of made my proposed rhetoric seem very empty. Within three days I wondered bleakly whether I had already lost the respect of many of my kids. What happened?

First of all, I didn't have the final roster of my class for a couple of weeks. Parents were hesitant to send their kids to the King School until they were sure it had settled down, and I was constantly putting off "really getting going" while waiting for the latecomers to arrive. When I finally did have the whole group, I had lost confidence in a lot of my bright ideas and was sufficiently threatened by the incipient chaos in the room to avoid taking action on those I still believed in.

Second, I was shy and somewhat introspective before my students. For many months the most embarrassing event in the room was to arrive at complete silence (as time went on this became more and more difficult to achieve) and then get stage fright because what I had wanted to say didn't seem important enough — at which point I would let the situation deteriorate again. For a long time I was influenced by an idea of James Herndon's expressed in *The Way it*

Spozed to Be — that of taking a rather passive role in the classroom, letting the kids work things out and letting things happen by themselves. They happened, all right, and I began to realize that such a technique could only work in very special circumstances and with a very different kind of teacher than I was.

Third, I didn't know what the kids were interested in, what turned them on. I was unable to "rap" with them to find out. It took a while to discover that many of them were completely resigned to school being an overwhelming bore — something to be endured and countervailed by the pleasures of sports, records, watching me get mad, and above all their fascination with each other. At the same time I was too sensitive and hurt by early put-downs of my ideas to see that underneath this, most of the kids had approached me with a clean slate (although it very quickly became covered with graffiti), and that all of them had a tremendous curiosity about the world, provided things were presented in the right way. I only really found this out when I started taking groups of four and five kids around the city (the aquarium, airport, skyscrapers, museums) in my car much later in the year.

Fourth, despite practice teaching and "methods" courses, I didn't know how to teach the conventional curriculum, let alone one more attuned to the immediate concerns of my students. I rejected rightly as useless garbage much of what I had been taught, but for many months I had nothing to put in its place — and by then it was too late. I was exhorted by some colleagues at the beginning of the year to "start tough," and then I could afford to loosen up and become more friendly with the kids later in the year. But I rejected this because I didn't know how to be tough; it just didn't fit my personality. Even if I had been able to do a good acting job, I didn't know the kids well enough to make it stick, and I might have hurt and alienated kids by taking tough stands on the wrong issues, not knowing when they were putting me on and when they were really serious. I naïvely hoped that the excitement of what I taught and my close relationships with the kids would take care of my "control" problems. This was theoretically sound, but in the light of my lack of competence it was a disaster. I was in trouble right from the beginning and knew it.

My basic problem was that twenty-five kids wanted to express themselves at the same time. When they did so, the noise and confusion were tremendous and upset the kids almost as much as teachers in neighboring classrooms. But when I tried to convince kids to express themselves one at a time I found it completely impossible to make them wait their turn. So although I didn't think of myself as an authoritarian teacher, I spent more and more time in the room bellowing for quiet with newly-acquired lungpower, simply trying to hold down the kids' energy. For many weeks there was no structure in the room but our mutual fear of chaos, no academic channels in which the kids could express themselves "legitimately," and no relationships between us that would enable us to work out the problem.

So the room became utterly chaotic, and all my energy went into survival. There were many fights, many furious confrontations with kids in which neither of us could back down, and very few classes that had anything to do with education. By Christmas there was a lot of hostility in the room. Some of the kids seemed to be saying, "If you can't teach us, at least let us have fun," while the expressions on the faces of the sweet, quiet little girls in the front row said, "We've been through this so many times before. Can't anyone find another way?"

Despite my efforts, the kids did have a lot of fun with each other. But I realized fairly quickly that the noisy peer-oriented classroom without good materials had an "anti-intellectual" tone to it, that in such an environment it was hard for a kid to do math problems or sit and read a book. One boy complained that reading was for girls, but the girls weren't doing any either. When I began teaching, I didn't have a philosophy of what a teacher should be. But as I became more and more threatened by the situation in the class, I found myself saying again and again that nothing could begin until there was quiet and order, that I must personally initiate all academic activities in the room before an orderly and well-mannered group of students. As I fought vainly to control the class, I told myself that if only I had a tough black disciplinarian sitting at the back of the class I would be a great teacher. As I thought back on my own elementary school years, I formed a picture of learning as a passive, absorptive process rather than an active, questioning, figuring-out process. It seemed to me that I had always done well in just this kind of classroom when I was in school. If it had worked for me, why not for my students?

During the year the answers began to dawn on me. Traditional teaching would not work for Grade 6-E, first, because I was singularly ill-equipped in terms of my temperament to teach that way, and second, because that had *not* been the key to my own success in school. I had conveniently forgotten the many deadly hours in my own education which I had survived by being more effectively intimidated by my teachers, or by daydreaming or getting involved in some marginal part of the subject that interested me. Being unable and unwilling to intimidate kids effectively (the job was a somewhat more tricky one in the King School than it had been in my schools), I realized that I had to find a totally different strategy to get my kids involved in schoolwork and help them succeed.

As I groped towards that strategy, there were times that seemed to be the long-awaited light at the end of the tunnel, but somehow it kept being extinguished.

After a few weeks there was a spontaneous rebellion against my amphitheater arrangement by the girls, who rearranged the room in traditional rows with my desk off in one corner. Boggled by the lack of structure in the room, they had seized on their traditional conception of "the way it spozed to be," even though they didn't have very happy memories of that either. (After all, desks are put in rows so the teacher can keep a better eye on the kids and keep them from talking to each other.) I had so little idea of what I wanted in the room that I put up only feeble and ineffectual resistance against the move. It was only later that I discovered that if I really wanted something in the class, I could get it; at this point I lacked both the conviction and the stubbornness.

The class began again in a more traditional style, but the vibrations from the young man at the front of the room were still as uncertain and lacking in engaging substance as they had been when he was in the middle of the amphitheater. The incessant talking and shouting continued between bouts of long division and grammar and spelling, and the serious fighting began. I found myself wading into all kinds of fights and tearing people apart from each other. One of the sweetest girls in the room tangled with another girl in the middle of the street after school one day. Again and again physical force seemed the only way to stop what was going on. There were days and periods of days when I felt I had as much control over the situation as a fly on the wall. I was hurt. In my tape diary I began to refer to all silence with the adjective "beautiful." My sense of humor faded as my shouting grew louder and more hysterical. I began keeping a batting average for the week, and found that only two of five days worked out to be what I then called "positive," while three were hell. In a full week, that made four positive, counting Saturday and Sunday, which was *just* survivable. I lost weight, and friends worried about me.

In October I came close to breaking the cycle. I discovered the duplicating machine and began writing my own curriculum and making it fun and exciting. The kids liked it, but somehow I didn't sustain the creative flow and we relapsed to the old situation. I discovered later that the wells of creativity needed to keep that kind of thing going were filled by good days and good feelings with the kids, and my well was too often dry. Conscious that I wasn't doing a good job, and having been put down by one parent in front of her daughter and the principal as "just a kid," I was hesitant to approach parents.

Then in November a friend put me onto a new method of discipline — a "constitution" of rules, a predictable system of checks on the board for violations, with set punishments for different numbers of checks. I typed up a set of rules (which I headed "Law and Order in Grade 6-E''), and read the riot act to the class. The kids loved it. They taped their copies of the rules onto their desks and behaved like angels for a week, delighted that at last I had done something decisive, while I tried one final time to make conventional teaching work.

But within a week their better instincts came to the fore (better instincts because they quickly remembered how boring a "well-behaved" classroom was), and they began very shrewdly playing on the system's weaknesses. Soon there would be twenty names on the board with various numbers of checks before we even got to lunch, and the sheer bureaucratic load of keeping the system going made me agree to start taking checks *off* for good behavior. This was of course the end of the system, since kids could be demons until lunch and then "act right" and leave school unpunished. Still, there were temper tantrums, howls of "Unfair!" and delegations of three and four boys storming up to the front of the room demanding that their checks be erased "or else." They had succeeded in making a game out of the system, and by the second week I was in despair as the "solution" I had touted so highly in letters and talks with friends crumbled into ruins. The now-familiar chaos returned.

Then one disastrous Friday there was another more encouraging or at least more democratic dawn of hope. In the morning my prestige had reached its all-time low. The whole class shouted together as I tried to report someone to the office over the intercom system and get help, blotting out my voice and giving an eloquent message to the people in the office. I had to give up, isolated and trapped with a bunch of gleeful kids. That afternoon I was totally surprised when the boys (the girls were in gym) began to talk earnestly about rearranging the room and putting some order into the proceedings. The upshot, after a vote with the girls present, was a return to the amphitheater arrangement and a forty-five-minute flurry of cleaning up, organizing, decorating, drawing up daily attendance rosters, and making rules and punishments to be enforced (corporally) by the president of each group. I sat back amazed, and didn't have to say a word. We agreed that I would keep order through the leaders of the boys' and girls' groups (there was strict self-segregation of the sexes from this point on) and would be free to go forward with my "teaching."

Alas, it didn't last. On Monday morning the girls held together pretty well, but the boys, whose leader arrived late and hadn't had enough sleep, were more noisy and chaotic than ever; they denounced the system and demanded a return to the former desk arrangement. I refused, but was crushed. How could such a beautiful moment evaporate so fast?

There were several other times during the year when these "revolutions of self-government" happened, when either the boys or the girls would suddenly and unpredictably take it upon themselves to get the place together. But we all viewed them with increasing skepticism, because, as became clear after the first one, I had failed to follow up with exciting and engaging work that would channel their energies. In fact, getting organized became an engaging activity in and of itself, rather than a means to an end.

A wider and deeper pit of depression opened before me. I broke up with a long-time girl friend and groped for scapegoats for my plight. One was the size of the class — if only I had a class of twelve, I could teach. Another was the lack of materials — if only I had better books, I could teach. A third was a group of six "troublemakers," among them some of the brightest and most attractive kids in the class. Realizing that I had failed them and couldn't operate with them in the room, I badgered the administration to transfer them to other classes. And of course I blamed the school (a prison) and the system (a dead end for the kids), knowing all the time that while there was truth in each of these complaints, the real fault lay with me and the horrendously poor training and inner preparation with which I had begun the year. I reflected bitterly on my earlier ideals and hopes, and remembered a friend's comment: "A bleeding heart deserves a bleeding stomach."

In December I fell into a rut of preparing work badly, not correcting and returning papers, not trying very hard. A Boston supervisor was aghast at my failure to "control" the class and gave me a poor rating, and the prospect of being fired became very real. My morale was temporarily boosted by a visit to a seminar at MIT, where a group of undergraduates listened to the big expert on urban education for more than an hour without cutting up and throwing paper airplanes. But my ego was soon squeezed dry again, and a series of friendly chats with a psychiatrist friend subtly began to resemble therapy.

Yet there were friendly days, and some marvelously productive lessons scattered among the ruins. I found that I was at my best with the kids working in small groups on more or less self-instructing materials, with me moving around helping individuals and putting out brush fires. When we operated like this, I felt very good about things and forgot some of the horrors that came before and afterward. But these classes were few and far between; there aren't many materials that work in such a setting (you have to write them yourself), and I never fully embraced the idea as a solution to my problems or got enough confidence to write a lot of stuff myself. Later in the year I broke the class into groups and had the kids push their desks together, but the groups caused more problems than they solved. Again, the problem was a lack of engaging substance. It was only in my second year that I discovered how close I had come to a really good solution to the whole situation.

Around Christmas, I began to weary of the shouting kind of repression and discovered an equally time-honored and effective method which I cheerfully overused for the rest of the year. Playing on the kids' notions of "way it spozed to be," this method consisted of feeding a class a constant stream of busy-work (copying and other very simple and repetitive tasks), smothering them in paperwork that had little academic value but that was vaguely satisfying to do. In my case the assignments contained just enough academic content and probing think-work (i.e., about five percent) so that I could rationalize it to myself, and enough chickenfat to keep the kids reasonably quiet for hours at a time. There were still regular explosions and confrontations, but this method took the pressure from outside the class off me and made the holding action more bearable. It also made me more ashamed than ever to call myself a teacher.

A further defense was to become more cool and detached, and in the process I began to regain my sense of humor. Attacks from the kids that would have brought me close to tears earlier in the year just rolled off my back now, and I laughed more at absurd and funny things. But then a sympathetic observer from Harvard brutally (and quite correctly) attacked my detachment, my failure to get mad, to sweat for the kids and fight harder for my program. What program, I asked myself? Show me one and I'll die for it!

Still, the remainder of the year went more quickly. I returned from Christmas to cries of "Mr. Marshall, I've forgotten how to behave!" but won a satisfactory rating from the Boston supervisor and was no longer in imminent danger of being heaved out of the school. (The Harvard observer visited my class on the same day as this supervisor, and observed that he had not seen "one iota of learning" take place.) I went through a spell of putting in four or five hours' work at home in the early morning, rising at four A.M. But I became discouraged when people threw away their corrected papers without looking at them, and realized that a system of more immediate reinforcement was needed. The class stabilized; I began to get involved in other things in the school, including a long battle for a reform proposal, which I wrote during the winter vacation (it was eventually rejected by the principal). And I began to direct my energies toward learning how to do a better job the next year. The man from Harvard had said that I had "lost" my class, and he was right; but I began winning back some kids on an individual basis with my eight-hour Saturday field trips around the city, which were enormously successful.

Then there was a three-week teachers' strike in May which completely discombobulated the year. School faltered to a conclusion in June. Somehow we had all survived it.

Winding in and out of these problems and crises was the detail of the year, the day-by-day experiences that were the flesh and sinews on the skeleton I have discussed so far. I kept a tape-recorded diary during the year, and sat down for two days that summer and listened to it all. What made sense in it I have written above. The rest was a kaleidoscopic array of faces and incidents that have no real meaning except in conveying the three principal moods of the year — despair, absurdity, and, occasionally, joy.

One large boy attacks another with a seeming intent to kill, completely beyond control. All I can do for ten minutes is stand between them and block, football-style, for the poor victim, who still gets a few ringing cracks on his skull.

With this same attacker, a period of hostility comes between us that lasts for weeks and is close to hatred.

My car has its tires slashed two days in a row, the second before I have had a chance to get the spare fixed, and I never know whether the knife was intended for me, my rider, or one of the other two identical cars in the parking lot — or just for fun.

I kick open a swinging door in anger and whack a boy on the nose with the corner of the door, provoking ten minutes of righteous fury and tears. Another boy stands at his elbow and eggs him on as I try to calm him down and apologize.

Huge eighth-graders saunter into the room in the middle of a class, trying to get a rise out of me. One of them gets me in a half nelson and rifles my briefcase, but is bored by its contents and leaves.

All the work of transcribing Martin Luther King's "I have a dream" speech is rejected by the class and I deliver a scathing and hurt lecture about how my best efforts are thrown back in my face. "Does it hurt, Mr. Marshall?" taunts one boy. "Always the same lecture," from a girl at the back. I never really figure out whether the idea falls flat because of the way I present it or because they are tired of hearing from white teachers what a great man King was.

Constant thefts in the room. Girls in tears of outrage because I try to get them to protest a little more quietly, blaming me for not caring. One day the room is ransacked during lunch; several dollars and pieces of clothing and a violin are taken. Another time seven huge posters of black personalities I had bought are lifted off the walls. In every case my prestige sinks lower because there is nothing I can do about it.

A flying Coke can causes a half-inch gash over a boy's eye. Later that day the same boy gets a deep cut in his knee from a protruding screw on the floor.

The littlest boy in the room stands enraged after I sit him down in his seat, tears streaming down his face, saying, "Go on, hit me, Mr. Marshall!"

From "sitting down" a bigger boy, I get a torn muscle, which is stiff and painful for six weeks afterwards.

Mother-oriented insults are hurled across the room, invariably sparking vicious fights. "Your mother plays around with Frankenstein!" "Your mother is a faggot!" "Your mother is dead!"

One boy has twenty-minute tantrums, and I have to hold him by the arm until he cools down, while the class goes from bad to worse. (But these tantrums become less frequent later in the year as he gets involved in an art project.)

Another teacher and I wade into a screaming crowd of a hundred kids outside the school to rescue two pugilists from each other. We don't succeed, the crowd reconvenes magnetically, demanding a rematch, and we have to drag one of the fighters two blocks away before the kids go home.

In the middle of a bitter confrontation between me and some other kids, two sensitive boys put on their coats and announce that they are going home because their mothers told them to if things got this bad. I have all I can do to keep them in the room.

Abruptly, uncontrollably, chalk of all colors whizzes back and forth across the room between the girls and boys.

I push a boy too far refusing to let him cut into the lunch line, and return to the classroom after lunch to find desks overturned, devastation, the floor awash with paper. Yet nothing can be proved; we can only pick up.

One day two boys break off the tops of eight desks, and over the weeks a few more are broken off. They aren't replaced for months, so that every time someone forgets his top is loose and opens his desk, the top crashes to the floor.

Kids roll around on the floor in hysterical laughter, falling off their chairs, pleading to be controlled.

A black guidance counselor denounces me as a racist who "hates these kids" because I shout at them and have referred one boy in my class for psychiatric treatment; she says that I am "just like Kozol," that I am "exploiting the kids" for my own benefit. But the black principal is constantly telling teachers to crack down on discipline, is vocal and physical himself, and urges us to use the counselors and psychiatrists available for problem kids.

A black administrator in the school scorns attempts at "creative" teaching in the school and implies that white teachers who make their classes "fun" are keeping black kids from learning the basic skills and thereby holding them down. But the black observer from Harvard chides me for not making more creative departures from the set curriculum, not being clever and creative enough to keep one book of lesson plans for visits by superiors and supervisors, another for *real* teaching. I am confused until I realize that race is not the issue.

There are days when I return to the room after dismissal and punch the wall hard three or four times, or hurl a piece of chalk smashing down the corridor.

I get "held up" in the corridor by a wild kid with a small tear-gas sprayer, and he orders me melodramatically to release the boy I was taking to detention. Somehow I knock the sprayer out of his hand, get his arm up behind his back, and take him to the office. He never threatens me again, but always greets me as "Dennis the Menace."

Again and again I have a sickening feeling when a confrontation in class goes against me and I know I am losing control but can't back down and I know I shouldn't have been stupid enough to get into it in the first place. Sometimes I call the office and for some reason no one comes to help me.

One morning I am livid, standing at the front of the room surrounded by a nightmare, shouting, "This class is out of sight! You don't deserve to be taught until you shut up!"

The first day I administer a standardized achievement test, the kids hate every minute. They struggle through, doing poorly, throwing down pencils in frustration, completing only half or a quarter of the test by the time I stop them. (One boy, who fills out the whole test at random, making pretty patterns on the answer sheet, scores in the middle of the class when the results come back.) After the tests, pandemonium breaks out. Chunks of eraser sail around the room, hitting me in the back when I turn to write on the board. One boys cries in fury, half-crouched, for five full minutes. Another runs out of the room when someone hits him. A third boy is bullied into tears just before lunch and for a while is afraid to go to the cafeteria. Then in the afternoon an experienced teacher comes in and teaches a conventional lesson the way you're supposed to and all the kids are angelic. I sit at the back of the room, exhausted, disbelieving, and know that I will never be able to do it like that.

A sensitive, pretty West Indian girl is bullied into hysteria by other girls in the room because she won't tell them Spanish swearwords, and runs out of the room in tears. As I run after her, there is a deafening animal scream of triumph — of blood tasted, a person on her knees — from the entire class that brings two teachers running from down the hall. Stunned, I think of *Lord of the Flies,* of kids' capacity for brutality to each other. More than before, I realize that savagery is there in all kids, and schools must come to grips with it, not just varnish it over with scoldings and "'disciplined" classes and civics lessons.

After a lot of soothing and encouragement out in the corridor, the girl screws up her courage and returns to the room she never wanted to see again and makes a peace with her tormentors. In the process she becomes a tougher person; during the rest of the year, as she gets better and better at dealing with her peers, she gets further and further away from me and from her former role as a model student and "teacher's pet." That process seems to be what is necessary for survival.

Hearing that another teacher is cutting me up behind my back and suggesting that I should be fired, I am so upset that I can hardly speak. The morning goes badly, and I get into an unwinnable confrontation and try to shame the kids into silence by not speaking myself. The struggle lasts for over half an hour and I am just getting somewhere when a superior comes into the room and tells me it is time for lunch. Seeing the carpet jerked from under me, the kids are gleeful. "Don't you feel cheap, Mr. Marshall?" asks one boy as he leaves for lunch.

Early in June, as I step out of the school at the end of a long day, I am slugged in the chest by an unknown boy, for no apparent reason, and so hard that two ribs are separated and I am sore for weeks. Others identify the boy, and at the school's insistence I take him to court for assault. I have to leave my class on the last day of school to testify in court, but his lawyer doesn't show up, and on the way out I stop to talk to him and ask him why he hit me. Sullen, a large barrel-chested boy of fifteen who others tell me is highly intelligent but a "lost cause," he claims that I had grabbed him. I realize what happened: he mistook me for another white teacher (they all look the same), who was policing the outside of the school and had been rough with him a moment before I came out the door. It seems absurd to send him "away" for six months for that, especially since the place he would be sent to would probably make him even more bitter and alienated. I talk to friends and explore ways of using the threat of pressing charges to get him into a really good program, but am told that none exist and the court wouldn't cooperate anyway. I visit his home before the next court session, finding him in babysitting for a younger sister, and offer to drop the charges if he promises to meet with me over the summer and go straight. He agrees and his mother loves me, but the black policeman who helped me in court bets me a dollar that the boy will be in trouble again within six months. I am unable to see him over the summer because first he goes to camp and then I go to Europe, and I find out in the fall that I have lost a dollar.

The class is quiet and busy one afternoon and suddenly the girls are screaming and running around hysterically. A boy has lobbed an eighteen-inch rubber alligator into their midst. I am upset by the racket and get the alligator in my hands by using all manner of dire threats. But as I bend over and stuff the thing into my briefcase to keep it out of trouble, I burst out laughing. The kids see me and we have one of the friendliest moments of the year laughing together.

I get a call late one night from one of my kids who asks me whether my washing machine is running and hadn't I better go out and catch it.

Another caller, more persistent, is a girl who rings me (and is still doing so), sometimes three or four times a day, and puts the phone up against a radio playing a Beatles song. Sometimes she herself sings; other times she wants to talk.

A boy in the class, his pride hurt by the principal, mutters about getting his cousin who plays for the New York Giants to come up and "take care of that man."

Several girls decide to change their names and refuse to answer to their real names for a week.

One girl who periodically flies into an incredible act of being a "hopped-up, doped-up soul sister" is so convincing and so disruptive that I consider turning her in for using drugs.

I confiscate a Danish magazine from the boys (actually they take one look at it and let it fall to the floor like a hot potato) and find in it some of the world's most incredible pornography in living color.

Three girls unburden themselves of complaints about me and get a round of applause from the boys after every pouting tirade.

A dictionary arches across the room into the wastepaper basket.

Little notes on my desk from the "Green Phantom" advise me on the merits of a brand of mouthwash.

When real silence suddenly happens, everyone looks up to see what has happened or who has come in.

We have a wild party in the room at Thanksgiving. One boy circulates a rumor that he has some Scotch in his Coke bottle and is instantly surrounded by a screaming mob, twenty cups outstretched.

Our candidate for the Student Council practices his speech in front of the class and is booed and hooted and pelted with books and paper airplanes until he retreats into a closet, from whence he meekly sticks out a little "V" sign.

One day I write on the board in the middle of a bunch of routine Social Studies questions, "If an electric train is going east and the wind is blowing west, which way does the smoke blow? One girl, like a good union member, refuses to answer it because "it ain't in the book." And the class is dumbfounded when I tell them after a lengthy debate that electric trains don't have any smoke. For once it's my turn to laugh, and the kids look at me as if they were meeting a new person.

One of the most angelic girls in the class calls me a faggot and congratulates me for putting on a clean shirt.

A boy complains that I am working them like slaves before the Civil War.

I say, "Where the hell is the eraser?" at the beginning of the year, and there are howls of protest and delegations march to my immediate superior. The third time I slip, I write my name up on the board with the malefactors of the day, and one boy raises his hand and says, "Mr. Marshall, you crazy."

The record player is blaring discreetly with my reluctant approval, six girls bumping and grinding around it, the rest of the girls standing around wishing they could dance like that, and the boys hiding in the closet. Another time when the girls are going through their moves, a boy sits back in his chair, feet up, puffing an imaginary cigar and says, "Great, great, put 'em on the Ed Sullivan Show!"

And of course the epithets: "Hey slick!" "I'm going to kick your behind!" "Forget you!" "You *bad*, Mr. Marshall" (which is a compliment), "Big honky liar!" (which isn't), "Hey square!" "Oh, that's cold-hearted!" and "My father's going to come up here and knock your glasses off!"

An incredibly close friendship develops between two girls. It lasts idyllically for months with only occasional blow-ups. One of them writes on her folder in huge letters: "Susan is my friend!"

Girls pore for hours over a book on childbirth and the facts of life, reading and understanding more than they have in school material in months.

We have a Christmas party, and the room is beautifully decorated with tinsel and streamers and snowflakes on the windows and a huge lighted Santa, complete with napkins and presents.

Kids spontaneously play the guessing game ("I'm thinking of something that's . . .") and keep themselves organized for an entire period without my interfering.

One boy writes a long story about how he and I go to Alcatraz for killing too many women and I die in prison and he lives out his life near my grave. It's confusing and troubling, but also strangely touching.

The class makes a large and superb scale model of Government Center in Boston over a period of months with their art teacher, and it is the pride of the school and is eventually put on display in Boston school headquarters downtown.

A group of boys makes up its own play and practices it endlessly. A king receives a panting messenger who says that the people are starving and the king says, "You got any proof of that?" (He doesn't.) "Off with his head!" The girls also do plays, and one substitute who covers the class for a period while I am in the office is terribly impressed by their eagerness to put one on for him instead of giving him a hard time like some other classes. (This was one of the few moments during the year when I felt that I was doing something right.)

Beautiful pieces of writing flow from the most unlikely people, despite terrific discipline problems in these rather unstructured Creative Writing classes.

There are periods when everyone is working happily away in little groups and noise is at a moderate hum, and I am able to move around and help people individually.

We have an intense Moratorium Day in October with Vietnam Geography, Vietnam History, Vietnam Spelling, and Vietnam Math (the cost of the war per second). It is possibly the most interconnected and rigorous day of the entire year, and the kids dig it.

From my casual mention of man's evolution from the apes, the fundamentalists in the class arise as one, full of righteous anger that I should doubt the word of God, and quite ready to insult me and that guy Darwin. We have a long and very heated discussion, which convinces nobody, but it is one of the few really excited exchanges on an academic topic all year. Only later do I realize that some of the kids might have been upset because they think the idea of being descended from apes is a racist one aimed at them.

We have a series of exciting inductive lessons on the parts of speech, working backward from the idea of a certain kind of word, writing scores of examples on the board, and finally giving that kind of word a name and forming a definition. We fill three blackboards with adjectives describing the word *policeman*.

And there is a magic moment when I return from the abortive court hearing on the last day of school, minutes before the final dismissal, and the whole class cheers.

Clearly, much of the story of my first year at the King School revolves around or touches on the issue of "discipline" and "control" of the kids. Why did I have so much trouble? The answer is that I brought the constant discipline crisis upon myself by not having anything much to give the class. They gave me many chances to produce — indeed, I was amazed by their tolerance — so the story of my first year was one of many opportunities that I didn't know how to use.

But I only realized this later. In the heat of the battle, I became fascinated with the mechanics of controlling a class of dynamic, energetic, restless kids. I decided that effective discipline was partly a subtle emanation from a teacher or administrator, which kids were quick to pick up no matter what mood they were in. Certain people with this magical quality could walk into my room in the middle of the most unbelievable chaos and instantly be in control, with all the kids acting like different people. Part of this emanation was simply a product of experience and confidence. My "vibrations" were for months those of painful insecurity and uncertainty. I couldn't even find my way around the school, and I was easily discouraged from elaborately worked-out lessons by a negative comment, my momentum killed by one kid with a chip on his shoulder. As the year went on, I became more confident and experienced (also more hardened), and did better in such situations. At the beginning of the year I couldn't touch a kid without him shouting a "Get your motherfucking hands off me!" or something of that sort; as we got to know and like each other better, things became quite physical both in good and bad moments (although I never hit a kid) without their minding it. Dealing with kids remained an exhausting and touchy matter, but I got a lot better at it as time went by.

But I never got to the point where I could walk into a room and have instant docility, and don't think I ever will or will wish to. A friend who grew up on the West Coast once described something to me which I had never seen: tidal pools near the ocean, in which a marvelous and colorful variety of marine life flourishes — crabs, underwater flowers, and so forth — when the water is calm. He describes the effect of the strict disciplinarian on kids as similar to the effect of the incoming tide on these pools: the flowers close up tight, the crabs run into cracks and caves, and everything becomes still and colorless as the waves pound overhead.

Most of these teachers (who have to be distinguished from the wonderful, stimulating standup performers most of us have encountered at some point in school) maintain that this kind of atmosphere is ideal for learning. Others are more cynical and admit that it is simply easier to handle kids when they are docile. I don't agree with either attitude. Kids have to open up to learning before it will mean something and sink in, and intimidated kids are not open kids; they have become silent because they have withdrawn to protect what self-esteem they have from being battered and bruised. Such teachers may be able to write things on the surface of the students' well-behaved minds, but what will that mean and what effect will it have when the kids leave that classroom?

But during my first year I had nothing better to offer. Indeed, it can be argued that the vague and incompetent liberal is as bad as the repressive authoritarian teacher because under the former the class has no direction and the kids are subjected to the tyranny of their peers. My class was often like a tidal pool between the tides, with the kids running around and playing between bouts of repression from me and administrators from outside. But while this was sometimes amusing and always colorful, it didn't get them much further than they were when we started the year. The antics in my room may have taught many of the kids how to survive better in their rough-and-tumble environment, and taught me a tremendous amount about the kids, but I knew I had failed because I did not nourish the class with stimulating work and activities or control its excesses of violence and cruelty.

Despite the fact that I realized all this fairly early in the year, I felt trapped by the chaos in the room, the pressure from the administration, and the lack of materials into trying to use a system of discipline that was completely unsuited to my own personality.

After the breakdown of my original dreams of control through interesting subject matter, I listened more carefully to colleagues who advised me to "get tough," and even to kids who kept saying, "You're not mean enough, Mr. Marshall," or "Tell me to shut up." For several months I found myself emotionally conforming to the expectations of the system: the desires of the parents and the kids for straight rows, quiet, and studious busywork with the teacher leading and initiating all activity. I actually became quite good at putting on an ogre act and growling at kids, but they knew and I knew that however ferocious I sounded, I was a paper tiger. There was one kid who, after the worst chewing out from me, would flash a great big smile as if to say, "That was pretty good, Mr. Marshall!"

My own attitudes towards authority had probably kept me from taking the idea of iron discipline very seriously. The year before I started teaching at the King, I was in the thick of a two-week student strike at Harvard that followed the summoning of the police to evict radical students who had occupied an administration building. No sooner had I discovered serious flaws and instances of hypocrisy in a supposedly liberal establishment than I was called upon to be an instrument of authority for an institution and a system which I had been led to believe deserved a good deal less respect. And so I remember saying to a friend in October of 1969 that if I were a student in my class, I would damn well rebel too. In fact I was often surprised that the kids were not *more* vocal, and that so much of their anger was directed against each other rather than onto me and the school. This attitude on my part didn't exactly put me in the best frame of mind to enforce "discipline," punish kids, and harangue their parents about their shocking behavior. Furthermore, some kids could be absolutely impossible when pushed beyond a certain point, and one of the most valuable skills I picked up was to see one of these confrontations coming and avoid it fast.

There was another reason for the lack of "discipline" in my class. In the teacher-centered classroom, the attention of the teacher is at a premium, and if the teacher is failing (as I failed) to deliver *positive* attention to the kids, they will opt for horsing around as a means of getting some *negative* attention. In other words, it is better to get screamed at than to be forgotten in a corner. Of course watching a teacher go all red in the face is also fun, and they played this game with me very successfully all year, even after I became "cooler."

It seemed to me that the most constructive — or at least potentially the most constructive — force in the classroom was the kids' tremendous interest in each other. Yet most of my energy that first year was devoted to suppressing this interest and telling them to shut up. In the framework of the traditional classroom silence is a virtual necessity, and when I yielded to their spontaneous kind of discussion of something that interested them, the class very soon deteriorated into twelve people talking at the same time on five different subtopics. In short, I hadn't yet found ways of exploiting this constructive force, although I began to suspect that that was the key to the whole situation.

Clearly I wasn't cut out to be a conventional, stand-up teacher in this kind of school. I might have gotten away with that kind of teaching in a suburban school (and maybe bored the kids to tears), but there was no way the kids in the King School were going to let me. At many times during the year there was a real question in my mind whether I was a teacher at all. But as the months went by, I tried to feel my way towards my own style of both discipline and teaching. This process was complicated by the fact that *I* was changing as a result of the whole experience. I was being forced to abandon the luxury of a soft, understated personality by my demanding and often threatening environment, by being front stage center for nearly six hours a day. I slowly developed into more of an actor and a performer, more of an extrovert, and grew a thicker skin and a different kind of detachment and humor. Toward the end of the year, my changes and my manipulation of the tools of teaching and discipline got close to merging, and a coherent style took shape. But it would benefit my next year's class, not Grade 6-E.

The turbulence of my classroom, as opposed to the placidity of the suburban school where I did my practice teaching and my own experience in elementary school, is part of what some sociologists have called a class characteristic — relative orientation toward the future. Most kids from more affluent backgrounds come to school with their radar locked in on tangible future benefits. This gives them a kind of stability that carries them through the myriad of temptations in every school day, so that they can put off some immediate pleasures and put up with the boredom and nonsense that school often presents. Less affluent kids, on the other hand, have less confidence that their futures will turn out fine, that there will even be a future, and so tend to react more spontaneously and completely to their emotions and the things going on around them. They are much more likely to punch the kid next to them if he annoys them, go to sleep on a desk if they are tired and bored, get totally involved in something if they are excited by it, and tell the teacher he is being an idiot if he is.

Being more oriented toward the future is not always an asset. It means that kids from more affluent backgrounds are much easier to intimidate with report cards and punishments, and that the business of conducting a poor teacher-centered classroom, of simply keeping kids quiet, is that much easier to get away with. In less affluent communities, on the other hand, the sanctions often don't work or are counterproductive, and teachers are faced with a vastly greater challenge — to deal with the unstable and often undirected energy of the kids in a useful way, to use their great ability to commit themselves unequivocally to all sorts of activities and avoid the viciousness and self-destructiveness that is the other outlet for this energy.

Of course there are other ways out in ghetto schools, repression being the most obvious and busywork another. And not all teachers in wealthy schools cop out on the job of arousing and teaching kids. But the unstable energy of ghetto kids seems to me to be a pressure which will put ghetto schools out in front of many more wealthy schools in breaking with the traditional classroom and trying new and more effective methods; the chaos in many ghetto schools will call up for debate the effectiveness of traditional teaching long before many seemingly quiet suburban schools realize that there is even a problem.

The demands on ghetto teachers are qualitatively greater; as a result, turnover is tremendous and people burn out very quickly. But these forces, all these elements in the "discipline problem" that I have catalogued as my woes, are the same forces that compelled me to change both myself and my whole approach to teaching. At the end of the year I had freed myself of a lot of the baggage I had picked up along the way and was, ironically, back to many of the same ideas with which I had begun the year. But I felt that now I had the competence to make them work.

Three.

Life in Grade 6-G:

September

I came out of my first year on an upbeat, with a certain feeling of confidence and an idea of what I had to do. Over the summer, I made lists of principles and resolutions for approaching the new class (which was to be Grade 6-G), and wrote a magazine article on the past year that helped clear my mind of some of the distortions and evasions to which I had succumbed. But I knew that I still lacked something very important — a *method* with which to tackle the business of day-to-day teaching. My ideas and resolutions had to do mainly with things peripheral to the classroom, such as starting my Saturday field trips at the very beginning of the year, getting in touch with parents early on, inviting in more interesting visitors, and so forth. The question remained, how would I hold the kids' attention when I taught Math? How could I make English and Social Studies more interesting than they had been the year before? I knew I couldn't teach conventionally, but did I have a system to put in the place of traditional teaching? Was I really that much further along than I had been at the beginning of the first year? I knew that without a practical system of day-by-day instruction, all my ideas and innovations would be tinsel on another disastrous year, and I was haunted by dreams of sliding back into the same problems. So I read books and articles and talked to people in teaching, searching hungrily for a method that would provide the answer.

In the middle of the summer I spoke with a friend who was doing practice teaching at the Harvard-Newton Summer School. Her class was experimenting with an unstructured format and had some good materials from Philadelphia. At one point in our conversation she mentioned that a master teacher across the hall was working with a method called Learning Stations. I was immediately interested, because those two words seemed to provide the missing link in my own thinking, suggesting an arrangement toward which I had been groping.

I visited the school the next day and spoke with this teacher (Warren Chafe of the Wayland, Massachusetts, public schools), and my intuition was confirmed. The system he was using consisted of pushing the desks in the room into groups (learning stations) and putting worksheets in different subjects at each group, sometimes accompanied by "props" or games. The kids would then circulate around the room, visiting stations that interested them and doing the work at their own speed, in their own sequence. As the kids worked and talked to each other (there was a low hum of conversation in the room), Mr. Chafe and his student teachers moved around the room, helping people who needed help and dealing in a quiet, individualized manner with any "baloney" (as Chafe called discipline problems) that arose. Occasionally teachers would pull together a group of kids for a discussion, but most of the time the class was "run" by the interest generated by the learning stations rather than by the force of the teachers' personalities. After school, the teachers met to correct papers, discuss problems and ideas, and cook up new worksheets for the next day.

I was shown a two-inch-high stack of sheets that had been generated by Mr. Chafe and a team of other teachers the year before in Wayland Junior High School, and as I read through them I realized that they as much as the classroom layout were the key to the system. The worksheets were written by hand on purple spirit-duplicator masters, and were chatty and often funny, with large lettering, pictures, arrows, boxes, and rows of exclamation marks all over the place. The personalities of the teachers who had written them shone through strongly (which was a welcome relief after the impersonality of most textbooks), and the sheets dealt with catchy subjects such as astrology, kids' attitudes to one another, making movies (which the class had done after exploring techniques in the stations), dating, and so forth. It struck me that it was not hard to write this kind of worksheet, to take ideas from textbooks, magazines, newspapers, television, movies, and the kids themselves and to write them up in a fresh and interesting form. The sheets were far from busywork — they were a curriculum geared especially for that class, centered around its concerns and capabilities. Moreover, they involved the kids singly or in small groups, allowing the teachers to get out of the "control" trap and move around the room talking to individuals about the work or anything else that came up.

I remembered from my first year the times when my class had worked this way for a while and the times when I had tried to write my own worksheets. In retrospect it seemed that there had been several points when I came close to this kind of system, but fell away because my morale was in such bad shape and because I didn't have a model like this to follow or a feeling that other people had been successful with this kind of system. Now the idea of turning out five or six worksheets a day seemed much less threatening, and I was sure the Learning Station system was the key to getting out of the constant discipline crisis. At the very least it decentralized the class and got away from the *need* to struggle for quiet and fight the kids' energy and interest in each other.

I talked to Mr. Chafe and his student teachers about trying a system like this in the King School, and they were encouraging but somewhat skeptical that I could do it alone, without the help and support of other teachers. As I thought it over during the rest of the summer, I wondered whether I could write five or six sheets a day for an entire year, whether I would be able to keep tabs on a fluid classroom with so many different activities going on at the same time. How would the kids adjust to it? Would their parents support it? How about the administration of the school? I decided that to run the learning stations alone in the King School I would need much more structure than was necessary with three or four teach-

ers in Newton. I decided I would form six stations —
Math, English, Social Studies, Spelling, Creative Writing, and General — and *require* the kids to finish all of
them by the end of the morning. I would try in the
four conventional subjects to cover every letter of the
conventional curriculum so that I would be well defended against accusations that I wasn't teaching the
"basic skills." I also knew that I would have to ease
into the system gradually, making sure that the kids
understood exactly what was happening.

The system I saw in Newton was heavily derivative of
the English "open classroom" — the non-teacher-
dominated, unstructured arrangement that emerged
in Leicestershire County in the 1950s and has since
spread to most British primary schools and has begun
to catch on in this country. But the learning stations
I planned to try in Grade 6-G were a good deal more
structured than the British model. In my case, there
seemed a number of compelling reasons for the adaptations I planned to make.

First, I was not at all sure of myself or of the workability of an "open classroom" in the King School. No
one I knew had tried one there, and people weren't
knocking themselves out encouraging me to do so.
I was in search of a clearly defined method, not a
philosophy of education, and so I was unsatisfied with
all the literature I read on the "open classroom" —
it was too vague in describing how to set up this kind
of classroom, how to prepare kids and colleagues for
the new approach, and how to deal with the many
forms of criticism that such an approach would inevitably face in a traditional public school.

Second, I knew that, unlike many English and some
American teachers, I had not yet mastered the fine art
of scrounging around the city for free and inexpensive
props that many English and some American teachers
have mastered, so my classroom would for a time be
bare of the many things ("stuff," the English call them)
— such as animals, games, books, machines, printing
presses, weaving looms, tape recorders, record players with headphones, typewriters, fish, science kits,
ant farms, and so forth — which are needed to run a
truly unstructured classroom. I knew that in the ab-

sence of a great variety of interesting activities for the kids to do around the room, my "open classroom" would quickly degenerate into open warfare.

Third, I was well aware of the legitimate demands in the black community for *results* in the three Rs. I knew that the suspicion of white liberals "experimenting" with black children was such that I could not afford to be accused of dillydallying around with a "permissive" classroom that did not have a very visible and effective effort to teach the basic skills needed to get kids into high school and college. I simply couldn't tell a parent that the development of her child's soul in an idealistic "open classroom" was more important than his getting ready for some of the harsh realities that lay ahead (including the strong likelihood that he would be back in a traditional class the year after I taught him). Unstructured classrooms are easier to implement in upper-middle-class communities, both because of the future-orientation in the kids mentioned earlier, and because parents are accustomed to their children succeeding and are thus more receptive to new departures. Under the surface of the educational conservatism of most black parents there is a real openness to new ideas, but only if they can be shown to be *effective*. At the moment there is little hard evidence that the "open classroom" produces results.

Fourth, I knew that my school's administration would take a dim view of noise and movement in my classroom unless it had a very clearly defined objective and could be defended in the light of conventional as well as innovative goals. Even with sympathetic administrators, there would be a need to make it easier for them to defend my class to less appreciative teachers and parents. The more honest proponents of the "open classroom" (notably Gloria Channon in her book *Homework*) admit that there is a fairly agonizing period of sheer chaos that lasts for a couple of months while the kids adapt to the absence of external discipline and learn to control themselves — while they become more interested in the activities around the room than in exploiting the freedom of the system and raising hell. The self-discipline that eventually emerges from this process is probably much more

lasting than what comes from a more structured setting, but I knew that my school and the kids' parents
did not think there was enough evidence of the merits of the "open classroom" to wait through a period
like this, let alone support me during it. Moreover, I
wondered whether *I* could take it without that support. Finally, I discovered that most of the thinking
about the open classroom dealt with the earlier
grades, that there was little theory, let alone a specific
program, dealing with the upper elementary grades.

Through the rest of the summer, my initial feeling that
the modified learning stations were the answer to all
my problems persisted, helped along by the sure
knowledge that if they weren't the solution, I was in
serious trouble. In my more confident moments I
imagined that doing the stations would be so much
fun for the kids that I could deal with discipline problems simply by threatening to take the troublemakers
out of circulation for the morning and have them do
something boring like copying. I also had dreams of
my plans crumbling into hair-pulling, chalk-throwing
chaos again.

One thing that remained unclear was what I would do
with the rest of the day, after the stations were finished. I knew I would have to do some conventional
teaching, partly to cover subjects that did not lend
themselves to being taught through worksheets and
individual conferences, partly to placate people in the
school who would undoubtedly be hostile to the
learning stations. I had no idea what I would do about
this problem.

Soon enough, school opened and a new group of shy,
curious boys and girls, twenty-three of them black
and two West Indian, walked into my room, quietly
appraising me and each other. This time I was ready
for them. The desks were arranged in six groups
spread around the room with about six desks in each
group (this left a number of empty desks, which gave
us greater flexibility). As the kids came in, I showed
each of them to a desk with a white sticker with his
name and station number on it (I had arranged the
class around the room in alphabetical order, with

boys and girls integrated). I then gave them a lengthy questionnaire about themselves and their previous experiences in school. When everyone had arrived, I gave a short speech explaining the idea of the learning stations and why the desks weren't in rows like they were supposed to be, and promised that in a couple of weeks, when we had got to know each other better, we would start to circulate around the room and have a lot more freedom. I also told them that starting that Saturday, there would be field trips for groups of four or five until everyone in the class had gone on one.

The kids seemed impressed, but were clearly reserving judgment until they could satisfy themselves that I wasn't a complete phony or another incompetent liberal. At this point the class was a sea of unknown faces to me, and I set about trying to learn something about each student. But there was a more urgent job. Knowing how important the first few weeks of deceptive quiet (the "honeymoon") were in impressing the kids and setting the tone for the year, I threw myself into the best conventional teaching I could manage in order to try and win the kids' respect by conventional criteria before I tried to establish my own. I also added a number of less conventional "frills," designed to break down barriers and establish myself and the class as something special.

The first of these was the way we decorated the room. I began the year with the room completely bare, in all its institutional-green splendor. On the second day, I suggested to the girls that perhaps we should do something about decorating it, and they had lots of ideas. Over the next few weeks, I spent around twenty-five dollars of my own money buying large black-and-white personality posters of black heroes, a number of smaller color posters with quotations and pictures of Martin Luther King and the Kennedys, and, as an afterthought, a large full-color poster of Spiro Agnew. The girls helped put up the posters and some other material they clipped out of newspapers and magazines, and the room was transformed. We got a "bad" reputation (meaning groovy, as in, "Hey Mr. Marshall, you got a *bad* room!") around the school and the kids enjoyed the feeling. At first people spent

Godfrey Cambridge - comedian, movie star

a lot of time looking at the posters and I did some projects based on them; but after a while they blended into the background and only visitors paid any attention to them.

The first Saturday, as I had promised, I took four boys on the first field trip in my car. I selected the four who I guessed would be the hardest to win over, and we spent nine hours together. First we went to the top of the Prudential Center and they ran around looking at the view — for all of them it was the first time they had seen Boston from high up, and it was a totally new experience. When they got bored with that, we went out to the airport and watched a few planes take off, then drove to Harvard Square and looked at all the hippies and had huge submarine sandwiches in an Italian restaurant. Then we drove south to Blue Hill, climbed to the top and looked around, and continued on down to the Cape, where we dropped in on a friend of mine and played some tennis. Exhausted, we returned to Roxbury and I dropped them at their houses as it got dark.

The results were spectacular. Word about the trip spread like wildfire the following Monday. I had demonstrated that I was going to make more than the normal effort, and the class was that much more open to me and receptive to what I suggested and demanded. Since the parents of the kids who went on the trip had had to sign a permission letter, they knew about it too, and I suspect that even before they met me I had made a positive impression on them.

For the next six Saturdays, and then three or four in the spring, I took groups on similar trips. The basic pattern was the same, although the others didn't go to the Cape and some groups got into the cockpits of jets at the airport. Some went to the animal museum at Blue Hill, and one group visited my apartment and went to a rock concert on the Charles. All the trips had the same effect on the kids and on me, and helped us to get to know each other faster and better than we could have in school. I tried not to use the trips as a cudgel to get kids to behave better in school, since that didn't seem fair, but after a while they became so popular that I occasionally succumbed to the temptation.

On the first trip, I got to know two of the boys pretty well. Larry thrived on the trip, and astounded me with his knowledge of the city and what was happening in the world. He came from a family of eight and lived right across the street from the school, and his brilliance and quickness were matched by his constant restlessness and tension. I soon learned that this electricity didn't find its way into his schoolwork very often; he had a lot of trouble with his reading and writing. His mother later told me that when he was younger he had had a problem involving right- or left-handedness and he had never really developed skill in writing with either hand, but it seemed to me that the problem went deeper. He was a classic product of the McLuhan era: his knowledge had come to him through listening to people and watching television, and his brilliance and quickness were expressed with his tongue and his body, not his pencil. He was fascinated by action and drama, and got bogged down in books, which never seemed to have enough. I found it hard to change this pattern during the year no matter what I tried, but Larry was dynamite whenever we had a discussion or a visitor.

Calvin, the other boy on the first trip, was a different story. He had a wry, teacher-baiting wit (a couple of days later, while we were discussing the birth of a baby to one of the passengers of the hijacked jets in the middle of the desert, he asked, "Did it come out through her mouth?"), and he had clearly had a tough time in the Boston schools. Although his handwriting was beautiful, suggesting a heavy emphasis on penmanship in the early grades, it was tiny and hard to read and his eyes were full of distrust and fear. Calvin loved every minute of the field trip, and the next week was clearly struggling with the mind-boggling concept of relating to a teacher who was reasonably civil. Still, all was not a bed of roses with Calvin for the first part of the year.

At the beginning of our second week in school, I got to know a third boy, George, whom I had diagnosed as a potential problem. I told him to be quiet as I tried to start a class, and thought I heard him talking a few minutes later. I put his name on a detention list and was stunned when he shouted, "You faggot!" at me. It was the first test of my authority, and the class sat back to see how I would handle it. Embarrassed and angry, I dragged George out of the room and stood over him impressively in the corridor, browbeating him: "Now what was that you called me?" Not in the least bit cowed, he replied, "I said *faggot*." There was little for me to do but say, "I thought that's what you said," and admire his guts. George claimed fiercely that he had not been talking and had been falsely accused — hence his outburst. But I realized from his attitude that despite the fact that he thought he was right, he expected to be taken to the office and suspended. For him, it probably seemed like a rerun of an old movie in which he played the martyred hero; he was already establishing himself among his peers as the boy who would be "bad" with Mr. Marshall.

I was puzzled. Should I conform to *his* (and the school's) definition of what a teacher should do in this situation, or try to work out my own way of dealing with it? What would the rest of the class, watching intently, think of me if I didn't do what they expected me to do? Did I have to establish myself first by the traditional standards of the "good" teacher and then slowly change them over to my own ideas? On the other hand, what was wrong with losing your temper at a teacher when you are falsely accused? How could I fault George for standing up for his rights, except perhaps to criticize his choice of words? I decided to try to make my own approach stick: I apologized for accusing him of something he had not done, and after a little more give-and-take, he apologized for swearing at me and agreed that there were other ways for him to make his point. ("I just got all mad," he explained). Both of us having backed down, I asked him whether it was going to happen again. He said, "I hope not."

As we walked back into the classroom, I wondered whether he considered it a victory, whether he respected me more or less for coming to grips with the issue rather than reflexively sending him to the office. Would I have the time and patience to talk out future altercations as fully? I was worried by the suggestion of a smug smile that played around the corners of his mouth, and feared that he had gotten the better of me. In any case, he had brought the class to a complete standstill for fifteen or twenty minutes and established himself with his peers and with me as someone to be reckoned with, which was more than most of the kids would do for many weeks.

The next day we got the news that our principal, the man responsible for "restoring order" to the school after its years of chaos, had been promoted to area superintendent. Feeling that this might mean a return to the previous situation at the King School, I was somewhat shaken and had a poor day with the class. As things loosened up more and more, I stopped everything and explained to the class why I was upset. They were surprised that a teacher should bare his breast to them, and were a little bewildered that I should be upset about it. Wasn't a promotion like that a good thing, especially since he was the first black man to enter the upper school bureaucracy? Later the same day things improved. We had a good discussion about the Arab guerrilla hijackings, and I had the unfamiliar feeling of the entire class sitting in silence, drinking up every word of the story as I told it. Larry was red hot, asking one good question after another, and I promised myself that I would not lose him during the year.

The next day it was clear that I would have to start the learning stations soon. Things continued to loosen up in small ways, and I was dissatisfied with the ponderous pace of conventional teaching. But I was still worried about some aspects of the stations idea, especially the possibility of not having a sympathetic principal (we didn't yet know who the new one would be) to protect me from an unsympathetic Boston supervisor. So I held back.

In the next few days there were several incidents that helped me get closer to the class. I spent an entire period chatting with the girls while the boys were at gym, and went to lunch with a very warm feeling about them. A day or so later, I visited the home of a boy who had brought one of the West Indian girls to tears by pulling her hair, and through the quickness of my response to the crisis earned points with both the boys and the girls. That afternoon, a wild boy from my last year's class came down the sixth-grade corridor with fire in his eyes and grappled with Calvin, biting him on the head; I waded in, tore them apart, and threw the intruder down the corridor, shouting after him, "We don't want you around here!" I even surprised myself with my ferocity, but the boys who had watched were impressed that I had defended one of them. And that Saturday I took four girls on a beautiful field trip and remembered for some time the expression on the face of one of the girls as she climbed Blue Hill in the brilliant sunlight. I helped translate the strong Trinidadian accent of one of the girls to the others, and later we went to Harvard Square and chose some more posters for the classroom.

With the new posters up the following Monday, the room began to look really special, but the day was marred by a reading aptitude test I had to give the class to place them in homogeneous reading groups (an idea that I strongly opposed since it broke up our class for one more period each day). There was a predictable number of arguments and fights after the test; I managed to talk one fight out with the participants with reasonable aplomb, and again didn't do what they expected — send them to the office. Later I tried to read out loud from *Animal Farm* and *The Old Man and the Sea,* but soon realized that I had chosen my material badly: George was disruptive as I tried to read to the boys, and it took some doing to get him to admit that he was being difficult because the book was moving too slowly. I realized that he (like most of the rest of the class) was totally unaccustomed to expressing his discontent directly with things that bothered him, but almost always did it indirectly by being naughty. I promised myself to try to be responsive to the reasons behind the disruptiveness of the kids and thus try to get them to state their grievances more directly, but it wasn't always easy.

My attempts to read these books to the kids was symptomatic of a rapid decline in the class and in my teaching. The fooling around increased; it became harder to get quiet for my projects and monologues; some kids tested my authority with alarming frequency; and I started to lose my sense of humor as scenes from the previous year began to recur. In the more successful moments of the "honeymoon," I had imagined that I might be able to do without the learning stations. Now, just two weeks into the year, the conventional teacher in me had been proven even more ineffective than I had imagined, and I knew that I had to introduce the stations *fast,* before I lost the respect of the class.

So I wrote a supply of station worksheets and, in real fear and trepidation, launched the system. I prepared the kids for moving around the room by having a "dry run" from station to station, musical-chairs fashion, until they were back in their "home" seats. Then I laid out the six station worksheets and held my breath. It turned out that the major problem this first day was my own apprehensiveness. I hovered around the room and fretted about the noise and other minor problems so much that I hardly noticed that things were going extremely well. The kids found the idea both natural and simple, and had little difficulty in adapting to it. There was one problem: I had insisted that they do the stations in sequence, moving around the room in a set order. This was one piece of "structure" that was unnecessary and somewhat disruptive, since the Social Studies station took longer than the others to do and created a bottleneck in traffic. The next day I allowed people to do the stations in any order they pleased, moving to any station where there was room to sit.

In the next few days I began to relax and enjoy the class more. Very quickly the stations became a pleasant routine for both me and the kids, and it was about all I thought or talked about for several months. The problem of the residual time when the stations were finished proved simpler than I had expected — I gave tests, had discussions, read plays, and so forth. The only difficulty was getting the kids to readjust to a situation where they couldn't talk and move around the room freely, and for the rest of the year I put a lot of emphasis on the difference in rules between the two kinds of classroom. They didn't find this idea very difficult and adapted very quickly when I announced that we were going to have a "conventional" class.

Over time, there were some important adjustments in the stations. The idea of having the kids circulate from station to station was a good one, and it helped them meet each other more quickly and feel at ease in different parts of the room. But it did not take account of their desire to sit with friends and form little enclaves within the room. For a few weeks individuals circulated around happily, enjoying the movement, the new faces, and the treasure hunt quality of the system. But soon friends were migrating from station to station in groups, causing a lot of confusion, and before long I was fighting a losing battle trying to get these groups to circulate at all. Since most worksheets didn't necessitate sitting at any particular station (unless a single map or book at that station had to be used or shared), it was easy for kids to run around the room at the beginning of the day and pick up all six station worksheets at once, and then sit in one place and do them during the morning. As more and more people started doing this, I realized that it wasn't a problem (although it represented a certain failure on my part to make the stations more intrinsically interesting with various "props"), and I allowed the permanent groups to form and sit together. Although this change made "learning stations" a misnomer for the system, we continued to use it for sentimental reasons.

There were crises at this point and later about who was whose friend, and periodically someone would be left out in the cold by a shift of alliances, and I would have to intervene. But this new phase of the stations (I still think the first phase is necessary) quickly became established and worked pretty smoothly for the rest of the year, forming the backbone of everything that happened in the room. Even with the kids sitting in permanent groups, the essence of the system remains the same: a class with six different self-instructing activities going on simultaneously, with a lot of freedom to move around within a long-range responsibility to finish all the worksheets; and the opportunity to do the work at your own speed, in your own order, and with individual help from the teacher or from friends. At the beginning of the day the kids would come in, settle down, look through their folders with the previous day's corrected work, talk to their friends about movies and things that happened the night before, and then collect their worksheets. For the rest of the morning they would sit in their groups and, between conversations and arguments, rest breaks and trips to the bathroom, singing, drumming, hair-combing, flirting, and the occasional fight, they would do the work.

The noise level during the station time was almost always eminently tolerable. This was because, although the room was a beehive of different activities going on at the same time, nearly everyone was involved in something that only he or a small group of people was doing; the activities of the class were effectively decentralized even though everyone would finish the same things by the end of the morning. My energy was spent helping individuals and dealing with occasional crises in a quiet and individualized manner that did not disturb the class. Beyond writing the stations the night before, there was little exertion in keeping the class as a whole functioning, but keeping up with the demands for my attention and help during the day kept me running and juggling jealous personalities every minute of the morning, and usually left me exhausted by lunch. It was well worth it, because the attention was delivered in a positive form, and kids did not feel nearly as much desire to horse around to get me to pay attention to them as they had the previous year. (They could, for one thing, get their peers to pay attention to them by simply going over and talking to them.) In short, the stations time was almost always a happy period of the day for all of us. We seldom had fights or angry confrontations during the morning, but when we did have problems, the class kept going, virtually running itself, while I dealt with them. The kids thrived on the freedom and yet most always finished all the stations by the end of the morning. Those who didn't were usually kept after school; but more than this and other

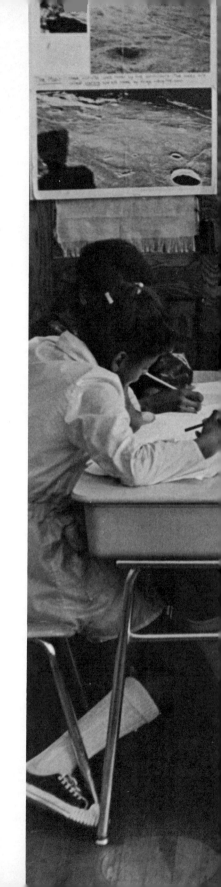

occasional threats, it was the stations themselves that kept both me and the kids working hard, the stations which, with their unique mixture of freedom and structure, appealed to all of us in a basic way.

As for me, the system was the key that unlocked my latent teaching abilities, which were little more than the ability to talk to the kids, to ask them leading questions, to give them appropriate hints, to prod them when they needed prodding, and to be patient with their vicissitudes. I became a low-key but effective personality in the classroom; I learned more about how to listen to the kids, and how to make them listen to me without browbeating them into silence.

We had stations from Monday to Thursday. Friday was test day, when people separated from their groups and did tests on the main subjects we had covered that week by themselves. Since I graded the tests and the grades from them were the only ones I recorded, this system gave the kids an incentive to understand the work during the week, rather than copying from friends or "cheating" on the correcting.

At first, my homework was also pleasant and not nearly as onerous as the teachers in Newton had thought it might be. I corrected the stations for each day in about an hour and a half, enjoying the Creative Writing most of all, and remembering as I went through each person's six stations how much work had been going on in the room during the morning (I estimated that our class did three times as much written work as more traditionally taught classes). As I corrected the stations, I wrote each person's grades on a weekly grade sheet, which I stapled to the back of each folder at the beginning of the week; this gave people an idea of their progress during the week and made it easier for me to spot stations they had not done.

However, as time went on the kids were able to work more quickly and my worksheets became longer and meatier. As a result the time it took to correct them became a burden to me in the evening and I sought other ways to give the kids feedback on their work. In December I tried having answer sheets at a table in the front of the room, so that people who had finished their work could use them to correct their own station worksheets. But this did not work out; the temptation to carry the right answers back to friends who had not finished the work was too great, and the self-correcting threatened the viability of the system.

Later I tried getting some kids to help me with the correcting, but this plan was hard to organize and had the same disadvantages as doing all of it myself: when they got back their papers most people did not look them over and see why they made their mistakes.

Finally I hit upon what seemed the ideal solution: I took the last hour of the day and went over all the stations with the whole class, with each person correcting his own paper and giving himself a grade at the end. This way I gave prompt feedback to the kids on their mistakes, and we got into many discussions on issues that were raised by the material, gained "practice" at operating in a more disciplined conventional class format, and I was freed of more than two hours of work in the evening that had not contributed much to the class.

Doing the correcting of the daily stations in class had only one important disadvantage — it was easy for me to get out of touch with how the class was responding to the material and what problems individuals were having with it. I found that some kids would not ask me for help even if I was standing nearby and was available. One of the most positive things about writing my own curriculum the night before was being able to "tune" it to the interests and abilities of my class. So it was even more crucial that I move around during the day, striving to talk to as many kids as possible, reading parts of their work as they did it, and keeping in very close touch with what was too hard, what was too easy, and what was just boring. I also looked over people's folders before we began correcting to make sure they had done the work, and still read and commented on their Creative Writing and the other more subjective stations myself.

Having made this adjustment, I found that my home-

work — writing the next day's station worksheets — was almost as enjoyable as watching the kids do them. I usually sat down after dinner and spent about an hour and a half writing worksheets, which left enough time to relax and recharge my batteries from the exertions of the day.

I found the business of writing self-instructing worksheets in the six subject areas much easier than I had imagined, and certainly easier than the task of writing amorphous "lesson plans" (required by most schools) for conventional classes. In the four traditional subjects, I started with comprehensive lists (gleaned from the Boston curriculum guide) of what subjects were supposed to be covered in the sixth grade in front of me, and paced myself to get through these by the end of the year. In the other two stations, General and Creative Writing, I thought up and borrowed ideas as I went along. (See the Appendix for lists of topics and sample stations.)

On a typical day, the Creative Writing station might ask the kids to write about a time when they were very scared (providing them with a sheet with lines to write on and an exhortation to fill them all); the Math station might introduce division of fractions with a short explanation ("You turn the second fraction upside down, cancel, and then multiply"), give examples, and present twenty problems; the Spelling might ask them to use words in sentences and then put them into context in other sentences; the General station might be an exercise in separating facts from opinions; the English a drill on when to capitalize; and the Social Studies a series of questions leading them to find their way around a map of Boston on the wall. On some days, the subject matter in the different stations was unrelated; on others, it would be closely interrelated, following a single theme (such as life in China or the national elections) through four or five stations.

I gradually developed my own style of writing these sheets, and after a while felt I could communicate very well with the kids on paper. The material constantly referred to incidents in the class and subjects we had discussed earlier, and was always affected by how successful the previous day's worksheets had been. A sheet from the day before might have to be clarified or approached from another angle or followed through in some way; there might be a need at that particular time for a "stabilizing" activity like copying Spelling words ten times each, or there might be a need for more stimulating, high-interest work like reading and writing about Angela Davis.

Writing my own curriculum offered great opportunities to share thoughts, anecdotes, and concepts with the class. Whereas the year before I had been constantly frustrated that I could not communicate with them about things that interested me (and vice versa), this year I had limitless contact with my students through the written word, and they could "talk back" to me on paper far more than would be possible orally during the day. The station worksheets unleashed my interests and talents on the class and gave the kids more opportunity to communicate theirs to me. I developed a much better feeling about what subjects would appeal to them, and when I saw such items, I plugged them into the stations and got as much mileage from them as I could.

During the year the Social Studies station, besides covering geography and ancient history, also dealt with the reasons for various laws, the morality of the death penalty, black history, religion, Greek myths, the trial of Angela Davis, the geography of their neighborhood, and many other issues. The General station touched on current affairs, rhymes and themes in rock songs, differentiation between slang and "formal" English (and knowing when to use each), the attitudes of the class on political and school issues, and a series of mazes and crossword puzzles. The Creative Writing station was a constant prodding of their imaginations, a daily opportunity for them to express their thoughts, fantasies, and experiences and then see them printed up in a bimonthly class magazine. By February I felt cramped with the original six stations, and added the Reading station. In this I wrote a few paragraphs about something and then asked a number of questions, ranging from objective to subjective. A few of the topics were: the story of an old peddler in Indianapolis, whose funeral attracted a crowd of a thousand; Spiro Agnew's stormy visit to Boston; Orson Welles's radio hoax, *War of the Worlds,* the plots of several movies, and so on.

Although writing the stations was not a burden, I did wish I could have collaborated with a team of other sixth-grade teachers; but this did not work out because of my own uncertainties about the system and the fact that other teachers had already embarked on their own programs. Clearly a team arrangement offers possibilities that I missed for saving time and pooling ideas and experiences. Still, I found writing the stations relatively easy. Drilling skills and telling stories with questions on them, Creative Writing topics, and Spelling words with context problems — these were very straightforward and quick to write.

It was introducing new concepts that was difficult, and it took time for me to find the level of the kids, learn how to break new subjects down into bite-size chunks, and present them one by one with an absolute minimum of abstractions and theorizing and the maximum of things to do. I added pictures and other helpful props, which I later withdrew one by one as the kids became more competent. When I did introduce a new concept in a station, I usually had a very busy morning running around the room helping the people who didn't understand it from the sheet; but I was aided greatly by the brighter kids, who helped their slower friends catch on. (All of the groups had a good cross-section of the abilities of the class in them.) If a ground-breaking station was well-written, most people only needed a nudge before they could do it themselves; if it wasn't well-explained, I had a hard morning and had to try a different approach the next day or pull the class together for a brief conventional class to clear up the problem. But, unlike most textbooks and conventional materials, most of the stations made most of the kids independent of me, giving us much greater freedom and flexibility.

With all the interesting topics that found their way into the class during the year, the traditional topics (the long division and syllabification and capitalization and nouns and verbs and adjectives) still got more than enough attention — indeed, the two kinds

The progress charts in mid-December

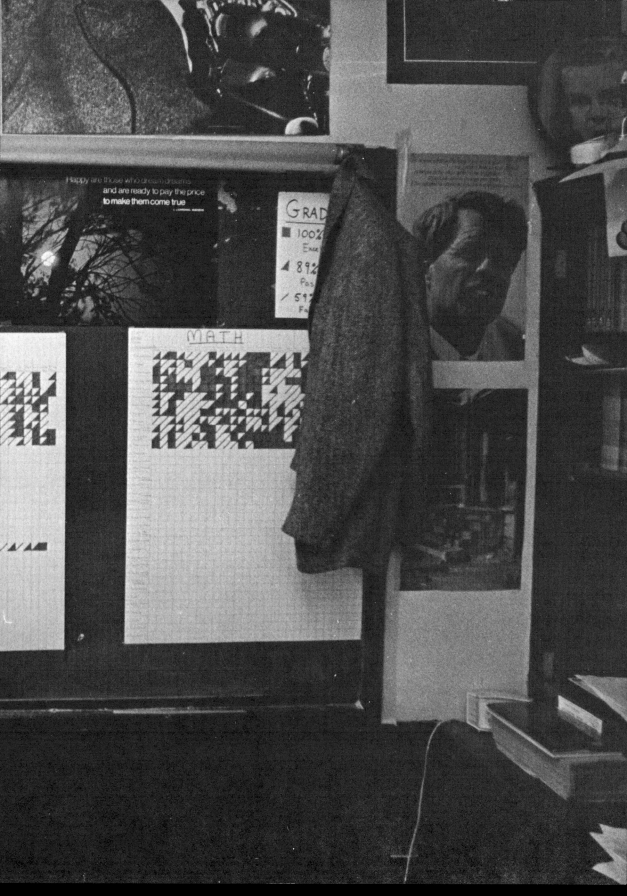

of work in the room fed on and supported each other. After we finished a "unit" in Math, English, Social Studies, or Spelling, we had the conventional tests on Friday. Test grades on Math, English and Social Studies went onto progress charts on the wall in three categories — high pass (a full box in red Magic Marker), pass (a triangle), and failure (a diagonal line), so kids knew exactly where they stood with respect to the year's curriculum, and could come back later to retake tests they had failed (I kept copies of all the tests in a filing cabinet) and improve their records on the charts. (The photograph shows the three progress charts in December of my third year.)

Using this approach, our class covered the entire Boston Public Schools Sixth-Grade English curriculum, the vaguely defined requirements of the Social Studies curriculum, the words "officially" designated as sixth-grade level in Spelling (as well as a lot of seventh- and eighth-grade words) and all but a few topics in Math (this because of a late start on the stations and the progress chart). We also worked through a great variety of more open-ended material in the other stations, and there were countless conversations, arguments, and other learning experiences scattered throughout the morning in the gaps between the paperwork. On the good days, which were frequent, it seemed that we had the best of both worlds — great freedom to explore other topics and interests as well as academic rigor.

Four.

Life in Grade 6-G:

October to Christmas

With the stations in gear, I began to get to know the kids more quickly, and, with so much freedom for interaction, a whole new dynamic began in the room. Not all of it was positive by any means. On the third day of stations, George and Calvin got into a rash of fights (although they were friends, there were powerful tensions and jealousies between them), and after trying to talk the problem out, I resorted to having their parents called up for conferences with the principal. I had very mixed feelings about going through the office like this, as I did when I rang the intercom buzzer for an assistant principal in a moment of anger a few days later. (Luckily it didn't work.) For a number of reasons, I had resolved that I would minimize contact with the office; when I did ask for help during the year, it was either an emergency or, as in this case, an unwillingness to sit down and really talk out a problem myself.

Within the class, I found myself walking a tightrope between being firm enough on everyone to impress the tougher boys and being sensitive to the more fragile kids. One afternoon I became aware of Eddie, who was in tears because I had kept him after school to finish his stations. He was a slow, deliberate worker, but exceedingly intelligent and philosophical. As I talked to him and tried to smooth the ruffled feathers, I realized all this and kicked myself for having become too inflexible in meting out justice to avoid hurting a person like him.

In the next few weeks, I developed an almost active

dislike for George (the boy who had called me a faggot), undoubtedly because he was the one person in
the class who was getting the better of me. When he
gave me the you-don't-like-us-because-we're-black
routine one day after school, I attacked him angrily,
reminding him that almost everyone in the class was
black, including the kids he thought were my favor-
ites. He admitted grudgingly that he didn't know how
my mind functioned, but he undoubtedly harbored a
growing dislike for me in this and other clashes. One
reason for this, I guessed, was the learning stations.

As I got to know George better, I realized that although he was the toughest and most militant person
in the class and associated with the toughest friends
outside the school, when he was inside he held to a
very traditional morality which the stations offended.
He would quote his mother on the way a classroom
was supposed to be run and the way a teacher should
act in certain situations, and was clearly disdainful of
the new arrangement. But if one side of his personality didn't respect me for not doing things "properly,"
the other, tougher, side was furious at the learning
stations. The reason I found myself disliking George
was that he was a master at baiting me and at organizing tacit support for various disruptions among the
other kids; and the reason he disliked me and the stations was that they took away a setting in which all
the attention in the room was focused on the teacher
(and therefore on anyone who challenged the teacher)
for most of the day. This meant that George had to
find a new "thing," a new way of making himself stand
out in the crowd, and he didn't find it easy. Although
he had a good mind and was good at Math, he had a
lot of trouble with reading and writing, and I often
caught him copying or stealing stations in these areas
from other people in the class. Throughout the fall I
was painfully aware of my failure to reach him either
personally or academically.

During the second week of stations, I got quite a few
visits from my immediate superior in the school, the
coordinator of the sixth grades, and I described the
stations to him in great detail. At first he was enthusi-

astic, and said that he agreed with the idea of having a great deal of work laid out at the beginning of the day and developing responsibility among the kids. Then it became obvious to me that he was coming under pressure from above to justify what was going on in my class, and he started to ask me somewhat hostile questions about the amount of movement and talking and fooling around that was going on in the room. However, two incidents won him over to supporting the stations for the rest of the year. First, I showed him Eddie's folder and was able to demonstrate that an abstract English station on capitalization had carried over into his Creative Writing, where he had written a long story with most of the right words capitalized. Then, a week later, there was a disturbance in the corridor outside our room which disrupted several other classes on the corridor, and ours never even noticed it (a week after this, the class worked through ten minutes of lunch before my stomach growled and I realized what time it was). The academic progress, the fact that I was covering the "basic skills," the amount of work that was getting done, and above all the obvious involvement of the kids in their work ultimately impressed him. On the other hand, he still sniped at me occasionally about my "permissiveness" and the mediocre behavior of my kids when they filed through the corridors to other classes and lunch.

Around this time I got visits from two parents, and was able to sit them down and describe the system to them, pointing out the progress charts on the wall and showing them a day's station worksheets. Both these parents and three more who visited the class later on were amazingly quick to shake off previously held notions about the way classrooms are supposed to be, and were very enthusiastic about the system. One of these early visitors said she had been bewildered when her daughter first told her that she had "stations" in school, but after seeing the class she said she liked the system and I later heard that she had talked to friends about how well it was working with her daughter, Helen. Lucy's mother thought I should be stricter and only allow kids to talk to each

other when they had finished their stations, and while I disagreed with her about this, I was glad that she recognized the validity of kids talking to each other in class and found her as enthusiastic as the other four about how hard the kids were working and the way they took so much responsibility on themselves. Anne's parents actually went to the principal to sing the praises of the stations — which was the best possible way for the office to hear about what I was doing.

Beyond the five parents who actually visited the room, most had no overt objection to the system and I always got a warm reception when I telephoned or visited them about field trips or problems. I found out later that some parents had spoken to the black woman who was the new principal about the fact that I wasn't using textbooks, but at this point she was convinced enough of the merits of the system to point out the amount of material I was writing and duplicating on my own and defend the system to them, so no complaints reached me. I was very lucky to have such an openminded and supportive principal, and she helped the stations gather momentum in the school.

In early October, I had my first visit from the Boston supervisor whose job it was to grade my performance. He was a different man from the supervisor who had been so critical of me the year before, and although he was quite conservative, I found him as receptive as the parents to the stations. Soon after he came into the room, Calvin (the boy who had asked where the baby came from) asked me in a loud voice, "Mr. Marshall, what's a homosexual?" Somehow I gave him a straight reply, while the gentleman eyed us both, and then was asked, "Are you one?" to which I replied, "No, are you?" After sitting in the room for most of an hour watching the stations, the supervisor came up to me and pointed out a group of girls that was sitting around talking, doing nothing academic. I produced Gladys's folder with all six stations immaculately finished, and he was impressed and retracted his implicit criticism. Later in the year, although he was still bothered by the messiness of the floor and the fact that I wasn't doing enough stand-up teaching, he said that I had developed the best system for handling the kids and teaching in the school; he gave me three good (but not excellent) ratings, which was what I had been getting at the end of the previous year.

Throughout this second year, I was frazzled by visitors in the room, whoever they were. I never knew which way they would look at the learning stations. Would they think the class was chaos with people doing what they pleased, and see me as a permissive fool who wasn't doing any real teaching? Or would they marvel at my uptightness about noise and horsing around and wonder why the class had to be so structured? I was unsure enough of myself and of the system that I was never at my best with visitors in the room. This feeling led me to block the windows facing out into the corridor with posters and pieces of cardboard to try to stop those who glanced through the windows from forming snap judgments before they had the stations explained to them or came in and saw the amount of work that was going on and the involvement of the kids. Even so, I was stung by a certain amount of disparaging talk behind my back among some of my colleagues to the effect that I wasn't *really* teaching and that I let the kids run all over me.

More sympathetic colleagues admired the system and were influenced by it, and sometimes used my station worksheets in their own classes. Although no one adopted the system completely, I was satisfied with this because I was concentrating on making it work before I tried to make converts. Friends also kidded me about my optimism and eagerness in a school which was imbued with neither quality.

During the year, the school did "loosen up" considerably from the disciplined order of the previous year. There was an increasing number of false fire alarms (sometimes three or four a day), which emptied the school into whatever weather prevailed. And there were several assaults on teachers, three fires (one of which knocked out the intercom system), and a rising level of disruption in the corridors from kids out of class and intruders from the community (in many cases "alumni" of the school who seemed to have nothing better to do than come back and make things difficult for the school). Combined with a certain neglect that the absence of any *major* disruption brought from the school department, these incidents further undermined the earlier feeling that the school was something special, and made many teachers feel they were merely holding back the tide in another troubled ghetto school. It distressed and exhausted the faculty to the point where a much-touted after-school hour became a time of infrequent and unproductive meetings and weary collapse after the rigors of the day (when the school department ended it later in the year, there was scarcely a murmur despite the extra money involved).

Different factions in the school saw different reasons for this drift toward instability. Some blamed the principal for not being as physical and tough as the previous one, and insisted that the school had to have a black male in charge; others accused these malcontents of not supporting the principal and giving her enough confidence to come to grips with the problems. Some pointed to a group of young white liberals on the staff, who were accused of fueling the fires by not being able to "control their classes." Others (myself among them) pointed to the impossibility of running a traditional "tight ship" much longer in the absence of some major innovations in the school, specifically a division of the school into "mini-schools" taught by closely-knit teams of teachers. The debate raged without any kind of resolution throughout the year.

About this time I became aware of Freddie, a handsome, mature boy who had seemed quiet and cooperative at first but suddenly began flirting with girls at a furious rate. The girls angrily accused me of not doing anything about him (although they were secretly delighted to be attracting so much attention), and I was pressured into calling his mother up to the school several times. This tactic worked with some kids, but not with Freddie. In fact, he seemed to enjoy the attention his behavior was getting him and fooled around even more. As the year went on, he became increasingly wild despite everything I did. At first I thought his antics were a simple case of puberty, and didn't take them very seriously. I was encouraged by the fact that, unlike George, he liked me and the stations. And I liked him, and assumed that he would settle down. But after a while I began to wonder. In early October his flirtations and fooling around in the class got him badly beaten up by a group of brothers and boy friends of the girls involved, and he nearly lost the sight of one of his eyes.

On October 6, someone in the office discovered that a boy who had been in the class for the entire year so far (and who had been on the first field trip) was not the person he said he was. He had come back to the same room that he had been in the previous year, knowing that he had been kept back. He found a different teacher in the room, but answered to a name on my class list similar to his own and was a member of the class for a month before the bureaucracy caught up with him. It turned out that he was supposed to be in the boys' Special Class, which was located in the basement of a nearby high school, and away he went. Throughout the year there were gruesome tales of the kind of treatment that the King Special Class boys were getting in that school, and I flinched when I thought that I had put up so little resistance to his leaving my class. He had been able to do most of the work in the room while he was there, suggesting that the tests which had placed him in the Special Class were less than authoritative.

Meanwhile, Calvin and George continued to pose problems. Letting people sit with their friends had generally positive effects on the rest of the class, but when these two sat together they grated on me and on each other; yet I could hardly demand that they separate while allowing everyone else freedom to sit where he pleased. They used up a lot of time that I should have spent helping other people with their work, and even this wasn't enough, since their demand for attention was limitless. I began to bring in a list of people who needed help in various areas every morning and make a conscious effort to get to them, but even this was difficult.

Helen and Lucy became outright fans of the stations. One day when I asked kids to make a list of their twenty favorite things on the General station, they both wrote "stations" and I was tickled. Both were bright girls and were undoubtedly in such a low section because their exceedingly large egos had led to confrontations with conventional teachers in previous grades. During the year I clashed with these egos several times when I was trying to run conventional classes. The girls usually succeeded in filibustering any class they didn't like, and some that they did like, because they insisted on being the center of attention and were very stubborn. During the station time, they seldom needed my help because they were bright and independent enough to do the stations on their own. But they still wanted my attention, so they played a variety of games, of which the most common was to call impatiently for my help and then, when I didn't arrive at their side at once, go into a sulk and refuse my assistance when I offered it. However, it was a pleasure to read their work, and they were great propagandists for the stations to their parents and other people around the school.

Despite the atmosphere the stations fostered in our room, it could not be an island in the rest of the school. The kids mingled with a louder and less contented crowd of peers in the corridors and at lunch; I was required to put in time policing various parts of the school and encountered this same atmosphere. There was one day in October when these outside forces converged on me. In the cafeteria during lunch, I was so provoked by one older boy that I nearly attacked him and had to be restrained by a friend. Then an unfriendly member of the staff, who had read a magazine article I had written about the previous year, made a scathing comment that left me feeling tense and depressed. And soon afterward I got into a bitter argument with a young colleague with

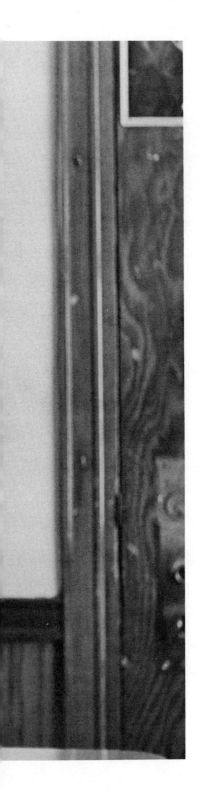

whom I should have been working closely, and stepped out of the school right after dismissal feeling disgusted with the divisions and pettiness of the staff and the obnoxiousness of some of the kids. I watched the seventh and eighth grades spill out of the building into the misty, sunny warmth of the afternoon, and then I wandered down to the gate by the street and stood with another teacher near a group of girls, saying nothing. The girls, one of them smoking a cigarette, another a new girl in my class called Mona, were listening to the Jackson Five on a portable radio, and suddenly I was overcome by the peacefulness of the scene — the girls moving gently to the quiet, lyrical song, the misty afternoon, the silent companionship of the other teacher. It was a magic moment, and it became even more magical when I noticed a chalk-written inscription on the asphalt inside a heart: "Mr. Marshall, Room 323, is a handsome dude."

Throughout October, Calvin seemed to respond to me some days and be a real problem others. (Monday was always a terrible day for him.) On one of his bad day, I accidentally banged Calvin on the head trying to get him out of a closet at the back of the room, and he came out swinging, out of control. It took all my strength and ten minutes to calm him down (this was one confrontation that the rest of the class did stop and watch). A few days later, he came into class late and was obviously very upset about something. He sat down at his desk at the back of the room, propped up the lid on a ruler, and hid behind it sulking. The girls left for gym and the rest of the boys and I got into a spontaneous discussion about the San Rafael courthouse escape attempt. Everyone was fascinated and peppered me with questions when they were not listening agape to my description of what had happened. Slowly Calvin's head appeared over the top of his desk, and a few minutes later, at the end of a dramatic sentence in my narrative, he was leaning so heavily on the top that the ruler snapped and the desk crashed shut. Everyone laughed, and Calvin had returned to the class. I knew why: the subject matter was tough, bloody, and relevant.

This discussion also fascinated George, and one of the best things he did all year was to retell the story to the whole class when the girls returned, remembering every detail; he did a magnificent job, and everyone was very impressed. For a while I thought he might begin to carve his self-esteem out of this kind of thing rather than disruptions and confrontations with me; but I was hesitant to present more than a certain amount of "militant" material. Perhaps I would have done better with George if I had been less uptight about parents and the administration and had talked about the Black Panthers more. But I didn't, and George slipped away from me again, this time for good. On the other hand, despite his visceral attraction to this kind of story, he might have been the first to tell me that I wasn't supposed to be doing that kind of thing in school. I was supposed to be teaching Spelling and Math and doing a better job of holding down his "bad" side.

At this point, in the middle of October, most of the class was getting very adept at doing the stations. The kids would charge through the sheets in concentrated spurts of work, and the end of the morning, when most people but not all had finished, began to present problems. I set up a "Free" station in the corner of the room and tried to collect books and magazines there, but I was never satisfied with the amount of reading that went on. Basically, the kids who had finished knew they had done a good day's work and were in no mood to do anything very serious. But when I put a checkers set in this corner, I got static from superiors and meekly withdrew it. Later on I tried chess without much success ("I feel scared playing this game," said Lucy.) So I took another tack, making the stations longer and more complex. I began to type them instead of writing them by hand, and found that this made preparing them a lot faster and enabled me to cram a lot more material onto a page. But this did not solve the problem of the ragged edges of the station time, and I sometimes felt compelled to call a halt to them before everyone had finished because those who had were causing too much confusion.

Near the end of October I finally got George to go on a field trip with Calvin, Freddie, and Bill. Everyone climbed up Blue Hill except for George, who stayed at the bottom and talked a young white kid into giving him a ride on his mini-bike, and then we sat down in a nearby Howard Johnson for lunch. Things went well, despite some stares from the largely white suburban clientele; but towards the end of the meal, George shot a wad of paper through a straw at Calvin, missed, and hit a woman sitting at the next table right above the eye. The woman stormed over and demanded to know whether I knew what these boys were *doing*. The boys were naturally gleeful, and it took me a while, until well after we had cleared out of the restaurant, to start laughing about it myself. The field trip didn't exactly work wonders on George's attitude towards me; the next Tuesday, in the middle of a brief sparring episode with me, he suddenly said, "You know what I'd say to you if you weren't my teacher? I'd say, 'Shut up!' "

The same day, Calvin had his worst outburst so far. He came into the class with an enormous chip on his shoulder, and scribbled incoherently all over his stations. At the end of the day, when I got mad at him for not doing his work properly, he swore violently at me and I dragged him out of the room, saying that we were going to the office. Suddenly he lost control, and I had all I could do for half an hour to hold onto him and talk him down. His eyes were full of an almost insane fear, and he seemed to be in another world. Standing by the school door, we watched some four-year-olds playing around, and I talked about them and how silly they were and how grown up he was in comparison. Slowly, tentatively, he began to get his bearings, and we returned to the room and cleaned it up together. Still in a state of shock, he went home, after we had both agreed that we wouldn't mention the incident to anyone.

My not taking him to the office had a very different effect on Calvin than it had had on George, because unlike George, Calvin was not playing games with me to get attention. He was really disturbed about something and I had inadvertently touched a raw nerve and then taken a great deal of trouble to make it better.

After this he seemed to improve steadily, although it is hard to say whether it was a direct result of this incident or of the field trips, the talks after school, and the stations.

The next day I had one of the first bad mornings of stations. I was introducing some new concepts, and the demand for my help was too great. It got more and more hectic until my circuits were overloaded and I shut down the whole switchboard and refused to let George go to the library or to meet other legitimate requests. At this, the pressure built up even more, and I ended up sitting on the class in a pretty authoritarian fashion. This happened periodically during the remainder of the year, sometimes when I made the work too hard, other times when someone's problems took me out of general circulation for too long and people who wanted my attention began to screech and holler, making the problem more difficult to handle. But for the most part, station times remained extremely placid and happy.

Having failed to interest the boys in *The Old Man and the Sea* during the periods when the girls were gone at gym, I fell back on the guessing game ("I'm thinking of something that's. . . .") that had been so successful the year before. These boys loved it too, and the posters on the walls provided terrific material for the game. We spent most of these periods for several weeks playing it, with the boys doing most of the "disciplining" and organizing themselves. I sat back and tried to figure out why it was so appealing to them that they could control themselves well while they played it. When I saw the smile on Calvin's face as he waited for the other boys to guess what he was thinking of, I knew the answer: you were onstage, you knew something that other people didn't and could revel in the suspense of waiting for the right answer and watching them flounder around trying to discover it. The game was superb therapy for them at that point, and I let them play it until they got more interested in reading, doing stations, and talking to me again.

At the end of October, I had a morning of strange contrasts. In the first lesson I had an unbelievably smooth class, giving an English test. The kids did well, and the coordinator stopped in and was impressed with the work they were doing. I was contemplating the boredom of teaching this kind of class all the time when all hell broke loose. A girl had had her pencil stolen and was in tears, and there was a fight. As I grappled with these problems, a girl from my previous year's class poked her head in the door, looked around, and said, "Hey Mr. Marshall, your class ain't as good as last year!"

The next day, Eddie was the victim of an unfortunate but common process. I was on cafeteria duty when an older boy started running around on the top of the tables and fighting. I tried to get him down, and he exploded, shouting across the room at the top of his lungs to another teacher, "Will you tell this faggot to get his fucking hands off me!" Stung by the choice of words and feeling the eyes of most of my boys on me, I confronted the boy, and the other teacher had to rescue us from each other. Back in the class that afternoon, Eddie stepped out of line and I leaped on him, storming to the door and daring him to step outside. He demurred and the girls revelled in the put-down ("That was cool, man!" exclaimed one of them), but when I saw Eddie in tears a few minutes later I stopped gloating and realized that I had taken out on him my embarrassment from the lunchroom incident. I talked to him in the corridor for a while, trying lamely to explain, but he said, "You hate me, don't you, Mr. Marshall?" and repeated the question for a few days afterwards. I was relieved a week later when he started coming up and asking earnestly, "You like me, don't you?" He alternated between the two for the rest of the year.

The same day, Calvin wrote this poem in his Creative Writing station.

One day
I saw

a snake
on the wall
and mice
on my bed
and saw
bats
at my window
and all
of a sudden
a king snake
wrapped around
my neck
and I
was
gone
gone
gone

While it was deeply disturbing, I was fascinated with the poem and gratified that Calvin should have expressed his feelings in the station. For a while he had been doing his Creative Writing over on the left side of the paper so that he could use up the lines faster and get it over with, and suddenly he sat down and wrote this. I put it up on the board the next morning and the rest of the class loved it and some kids tried to imitate the style for several days. Calvin's head swelled, and he wrote many other poems during the year, although none of them was quite as existential as this one. He also began to do better in Math, which he had hated, and he improved steadily. We had worked out a very good accommodation — he knew my limits and I knew his. He would fool around with the other boys, but when I showed that I had had enough, he usually stopped when some of the others didn't and avoided being punished. His hysterical losses of control stopped, and he often stayed after school and came in early to talk and do work.

The day I showed Calvin's poem to the class, things went so well that I had thirteen volunteers to stay after school and retake old tests on which they had done poorly. I got permission from the office to keep them, but as we were about to begin, a vicious fight broke out between Freddie and Helen; it was a real fur-flying affair, and it took all my strength to hold Helen down and get Freddie out of the room. The great testing session fizzled, and I never again aroused so much enthusiasm in catching up.

The next morning Freddie's mother was up at the school again and vowed that she was going to "kill" him, but as soon as he was back in the classroom his eyes lit up — he was irrepressible and in a way I admired that. The girls saw the gleam and when the boys left for gym, bombarded me with bitter complaints about my favoritism and so forth. "You ain't got no feelings!" said Mona, and the others said that I wasn't doing anything about "them boys," and that I liked them more than the girls anyway. I promised lamely that I would try to do better, and once again felt myself trapped between their idea of discipline and my own. I knew that the traditional controls didn't work with Freddie and only got me into time-consuming struggles with George, but I obviously hadn't found other ways of stopping their destructive tendencies, even with field trips and fairly close relationships. A few days later, when George called me a motherfucker at the end of a long confrontation, I sent him to the office in exasperation. But in this and all other cases in which I called in the office for help, he was never seriously punished, his parents never summoned to the school.

Soon thereafter there was a crisis with the Puerto Rican boy in the class. (The boy was taking a lot of racially-oriented abuse from the other kids.) His mother came up to the school and claimed that one of the girls in the class had been calling him on the phone and harassing him, and wanted to know whether I had given her their telephone number. It turned out that in his printing class the boy had made calling cards with his phone number and the girl had gotten one of these. The next day the administration transferred the boy to another class. A little later the other nonblack student in the room, a shy girl from

Grenada who had had her hair pulled once too many
times and said she found the work too easy, was
moved up to one of the academic sections, and we
had an all-black class.

Just before the Congressional elections in November,
we got into a series of discussions about the election
issues, and I sent a questionnaire home with the kids
to find the views of their families; we then used the
results to make graphs at the General station the next
day. Later, we got into a lengthy talk about Charles
Manson and the contention of one of the prosecution
lawyers that Manson had arranged the murders to try
to start race warfare. These and many other spontaneous discussions (about the Kennedys, the moon shots,
My Lai, welfare, Angela Davis, Malcolm X, subma-
rines, nuclear war, Spiro Agnew, the black protest at

the Olympics, and so forth) throughout the year fueled and supplemented the stations. They were seldom initiated by me; in fact, I usually found that if I tried to get a discussion going, it fell flat. Rather, the discussions happened when a group of people got interested in a station worksheet or something they had seen in a newspaper or on television. Then I could seize the moment and pull the class together. This seemed a unique feature of the learning stations — that we could have this kind of talk and then return to the work at hand without a great disruption or a feeling that it had been a "red herring."

There were also countless questions from individual kids, which I was free to sit down and try to answer on the spot. "Why does the moon go around the earth?" "What is a Black Muslim?" "Is sniffing glue dangerous?" "Why was John Kennedy killed?" and so forth. The thing that irked me more than anything else about conventional teaching was that if a kid came up with one of these questions during a lecture class, you had to tell him to be quiet and pay attention to what was going on. Now I was free to respond to the kids immediately, and sometimes involve the class in an impromptu discussion branching out from particular questions.

The day after elections, we had a sixth-grade assembly in which a young white man demonstrated and lectured on lights, and got me thinking about the issue of race in the school. It was an exciting show, including psychedelic, pulsating lights moving and changing in time to some rock music. But the show flopped when the man volunteered the comment that black was not in fact a color but the absence of color, while white was the combination of all colors. "It's a mistake to say that black is beautiful," he said, "because black is not a color." While this may be true of light, the opposite is true of pigments, where *black* is clearly the combination of all colors; but the kids didn't know that and turned icy cold.

When we got back to the room, I started a discussion about color and for once got it off the ground. I explained the difference between lights and pigments, and asked them whether they thought the man was a racist to make the remark. They thought he probably was, and were remarkably receptive to hearing all this from me. I had put myself on their side of a racial question and they had tentatively accepted me there.

Later in the year when a substitute nurse made a remark, while she weighed and measured them, about the way the girls smelled, they exploded (typically, they did so in an indirect manner, fooling around and messing up the room rather than coming out and saying what had outraged them). This led to one of the tensest moments of the year and brought me to tears, but again I put myself on their side. I gladly reported the nurse, and was backed up by the principal — and the girls appreciated it.

Aside from some glib rhetoric from some of the boys, race was never an issue that came between me and the kids. Having an all-black class helped because I couldn't be accused of favoring or punishing someone because of his race. There *was* racism among the kids towards the fifteen or so Puerto Rican kids in the school, and many liberal teachers were horrified to hear the kids mouthing familiar racist slogans in talking about them.

The social pecking order of Boston is laid out along Blue Hill Avenue, which runs near the school, following the pattern of migration out of the ghetto. From the suburbs inward, the order is: WASPS, Irish Catholics, Jews, Negroes, and finally Puerto Ricans, who are indeed the new "'niggers" of the city and are even more so since they lack the level of political organization, unity, and academic backup that the blacks now enjoy. I tried to impress this on kids during the year, but was fighting strongly rooted attitudes and demonstrating my own naïveté as to how a pecking order works. The importance of this to the kids is demonstrated by the fact that race ranks with motherhood and masculinity in the ultimate King School insult, "Your mother is a Puerto Rican faggot."

As for their racial attitudes towards teachers, the kids seemed to make judgments on the basis of personality and competence rather than race. For them, the criterion of respect was whether a teacher was "together," not necessarily in the liberal connotation of that word. A traditional teacher who was competent and sure of himself did better than a vacillating radical, even if the latter's views on political issues were "right on." The kids could be equally scathing and disruptive to black and white teachers who they felt were doing poorly and whom they didn't like. Teachers who gained the affection and confidence of the kids could discuss any issue and be very physical with them, whatever color they were, while for those who didn't, the common refrain was, "Get your mother-fucking hands off me!"

These attitudes towards teachers and the problems faced by white and Puerto Rican students in the school suggest that the black kids are more racially tolerant of adults than of their peers, at least within the competitive atmosphere of the school. This is probably because they themselves have been subjected to abuse on racial and class issues and are pressured to pass it on down the pecking order or take it out on whites (but not on white teachers, since that would get them in too much trouble). Another reason is that the dynamics of most classrooms present situations where tensions and particularly jealousies can readily be blamed on race. Even among themselves, the kids bantered constantly about race, playing around with the implications of the issues involved. Recently "nigger" has become almost as common a term of address among some kids as "man," and there was a constant harping on the issue of welfare — "Your mother eats welfare chopped meat!" "He wears hand-me-down drawers!" "Your clothes come from Goodwill!" These remarks were often hurled around disputes, and almost invariably sparked vicious fights.

What is the position of white teachers in schools like the King? A colleague said to me on a bad day in the fall of my second year that white teachers had no place in a school like the King, and I disagreed vehemently. It seemed to me that a dynamic and successful white teacher who made kids feel proud of themselves and taught effectively was as good as a similar black teacher. But later in the year I changed my mind. I decided that although there is a definite place for competent white teachers now — while the short-

age of available and "qualified" blacks is so acute —
the time will come in the next few years when it will
be more important that the kids have black teachers in
their classrooms to teach them and act as models and
examples of success. The trend towards black staffing
and administration and some degree of community
control in ghetto schools is unmistakable. Perhaps I
am working myself out of a job.

Of course the black administrators and teachers in the
King School do not have an instant ticket to success
with the kids. Many black staff members are upwardly
mobile and are less comfortable with the language,
mores, music, and political attitudes of the kids than
are many young white teachers. But this kind of dis-
parity may not last very long.

There is a certain amount of rhetoric in the school
about blacks "getting it together" by themselves without the help of whites, but the reality is more a matter
of internecine class struggles (as between the kids on
the issue of welfare) and occasionally a grossly inap-
propriate use of the issue that tends to discredit it.
Sometimes, for example, when assemblies are going
badly and becoming noisy and chaotic, a black administrator will get up and talk about black folks getting
themselves together and not acting this way in front
of whites, and invariably the kids will be somewhat
embarrassed, as if they think it an unfair use of the
argument to shut them up, and continue doing what
they were doing.

Once late that second year when someone shouted
this rationale through a loudspeaker in the middle of
a full-scale riot at an outdoor field day, it was almost
a joke. To the outsider, of course, it might seem that
everyone in the all-black King School is in the same
boat, but within it, it is obvious that society has created all sorts of divisions which black people are only
now being given the opportunity to deal with at all.

Within the staff, the issue of race was much more
complicated. Because so many of the liberal teachers
in the school were white, one form of attack to which
we were subjected from the more conservative black
teachers was that we were "permissive white do-
gooders," who felt sorry for the kids, patronized

them, and weren't giving them the kind of education they needed. Some of the bitterness of those who felt this way was accurately represented in an anonymous letter I received in the fall in response to the magazine article I wrote about my first year:

Dear Sir:
Your article clearly shows that whites do NOT belong in Black schools. With all your woes and problems, you forget that the 25 Black students you "taught" have had another year robbed from them (and people wonder why when they become adults they can't "make it" in society). It is unfortunate that you had to "gain your experience" by stealing 25 childrens' lives for a year. However, Honky — your day will come!
One Black who reads the Harvard *Bulletin*

But race didn't seem to me to be the real issue in this attitude. If the young liberal teachers had been black, they would have been subjected to the same criticism by the same people for the same basic reasons, minus the mention of race. If I had been a *competent* white teacher in my first year, the letter would not have been written (although it also might not have been written if I had been an incompetent black). The *real* issues here are: (1) the actual competence of the young liberal teachers, which is open to question in some cases, and (2) a genuine disagreement among educators about what methods to use to teach the kids, and what they really *need* to know to make their way in the world. Is the authoritarian classroom the only way to teach kids? Is it failing or is it merely the victim of soft, "permissive" teachers? Do black kids need only "basic skills" to make it in America, or do their more basic problems need to be brought out into the open and dealt with? Is a classroom like mine, where the teacher seems to take such a passive role, capable of teaching kids at all?

Unfortunately these issues have never been discussed frankly during the years I have been at the school. (To do so would undoubtedly require full-scale sensitivity training, to which many of the teachers are violently opposed.) But they lurk under the surface in countless one-sided conversations and they poison the atmosphere. If something were done to clear the air and reach a meeting of minds (even an agreement to disagree would be a good step), some of the phony racism that accompanies these attitudes might disappear. Clearly the real divisions on the staff are based on age, ideology, and class, and there is a similar lack of communication and feeling of contempt on both sides of the fence. If the conservatives disdain our bell-bottoms, political views, and relatively unstructured classes, the liberals can be equally snotty about *their* upward mobility, bow ties, and preoccupation with "control." If the conservatives accuse us of being dilettantes, do-gooders, and draft-dodgers, the liberals deride the conservatives' big cars, parties, and "professionalism." The King faculty is not big on peaceful coexistence, and social gatherings do little to bring us together. Ironically, it may only be a real crisis that can accomplish that, and if we don't get together, that is exactly what we are going to get.

Soon after the elections in November, one of the prime mechanisms of class stratification, the Stanford Achievement Test, came to our class for an agonizing two and a half hours. I hoped that the constant practice at reading directions and doing work on their own had prepared the kids to take these tests better, and I gave them a pep talk beforehand. But by the end they were all going soft in the head, and several of the boys took refuge in filling them out at random or refusing to do them at all. I wondered whether I was not being absurdly uptight not to do what many other teachers do — give the kids much more time than is allowed and openly help them with difficult problems — and became very depressed reading the kind of textbook vocabulary and knowledge the tests contained.

Two days later, on November 9, the first batch of report cards came out; as always the kids grabbed them eagerly and most were pleased with the grades I had given them (which they deserved). I took some comfort in the knowledge that my grades would affect their futures as well as the absurd standardized tests.

That afternoon I tried to keep Calvin after school for some offense, but forgot that I didn't have the proper legal backing to do it (three checks in my little black book). There was an outburst of righteous indignation from the boys, and just before I finally backed down one of them said bitterly, "That's the kind of thing that makes me so mad about this place. I swear, when I grow up I'm going to blow up schools like this! Just wait till I get to college."

But when I did back down, we shifted abruptly to a more friendly tone, and they became fascinated with finding out what my first name was. Although I had told them several times during the year, they kept calling me Mr. Marshall — although a few times one of them shouted, "Hey, Kim!" at me in front of other teachers to get my goat.

It is significant that, although I talked to everyone in the class individually many times each day, I had only really come to know a few kids by the middle of November; the ones I have described so far are the ones who had succeeded in making themselves known in the crowd. The other kids realized this, and perhaps resented the fact that these few were getting more attention. Those whose personalities were less distinctive tried to find ways to bring themselves to my attention and be noticed by their peers. Steven, a quiet boy who had a lot of difficulty with some of his work, had equal trouble getting through to me and I to him, until one day in November when I got so mad at his refusal to listen to my explanations of a problem that I grabbed him by the cheeks and reduced him to tears. I felt terrible and spent a lot of time trying to make him feel better, and that was a real turning point for both of us: Steven had put himself on the map. Granted, his "thing" continued to be his brilliant imitations of James Brown singing soulfully and his furious drumming on the edge of his desk (occasionally twirling a drumstick and deftly catching it), but he also began to let me help him in his work and improved steadily.

I had less luck with Gloria. She had similar academic problems, and was also an extremely popular girl who was always involved in some kind of social activity. Through most of the year she would not let me help her. When I tried she just wouldn't listen. There were some very bright people in her group and she got a lot of good help from them and made progress; but to the end of the year I felt that I had not got through to her academically.

I felt the same way about Alice, who was so sensitive and quiet that I didn't talk to her very often and sometimes didn't put much pressure on her to finish her work — which aroused considerable bitterness among some of the other girls, notably Anne, who were working their ta.ls off all morning. But at the end of November, Alice put herself on the map too. Pushing into a wild crowd scene of 150 kids on the street after school, I found that several girls were trying to get a fight started between her and Mona, and although neither of them felt like fighting, they were both enjoying the attention immensely. But people pushed them together, and as things began to get serious I had to rescue Alice and drag her back up the hill into the school, followed by the entire crowd until the door slammed shut. Alice was also one of the great fans of the field trips, enjoying every minute of them and making some friends in the class while we were driving around the city.

Meanwhile I got to like Eddie more and more. In after-school sessions (which became less and less punitive), with him and his friends he often dazzled us with an incredibly adult vocabulary (which was unfortunately purely oral, like Larry's) and a continuing stream of one-liners. The current one: "I wish I was dead so I could come back and haunt people." And George continued to embarrass and annoy me. After I had nearly fallen down chasing Calvin around the room and had taken my embarrassment out on him, George said, "Oh, you're just mad at him because he made a fool of you." Perhaps I just didn't have enough of a sense of humor to get along with him.

At the beginning of December, a colleague put together a school magazine of kids' writing, and several pieces from our class (taken from our bimonthly magazine of creative writing) were included. I tried to read the magazine out loud in class, but did not realize that Helen's and Lucy's prodigious output had not found its way into print, and they were bitter and succeeded in disrupting the class completely. When I talked to their parents and explained the situation that afternoon, none of us could be very mad at them, and

Lucy's mother told me that Lucy was thinking of becoming a writer. However, this incident seemed to stop her progress on the Creative Writing station, and she didn't write nearly as much for the rest of the year. Trying to read the magazine had been a major blunder.

During the heated confrontation that morning, I got so mad that some of the boys started calling me "Mr. Red," and for a couple of weeks it stuck — a constant reminder to me to stay cool. But a few days later Eddie came up to me and said, "You know, Mr. Marshall, I like you," and I felt better.

Shortly before Christmas, George, Eddie, Calvin, and Larry started to come up to the room early, half an hour before the bell rang to begin school, to start on their work and talk with me. Although I was very busy at this point, I was able to talk to them a little and was secretly delighted that some of the toughest boys in the class were thinking of the classroom as a friendly enough place to make getting up earlier worthwhile. They continued to do this, joined by Freddie and Bill and later Tyrone, for the rest of the year. Some mornings I would be in a bad mood and they would be noisy and I would throw them out, but most of the time they would talk about television shows and get a head start on the stations and there was a good feeling in the room.

As we began to decorate for Christmas, we felt ourselves in the finishing stretch of the first part of the year. Working mainly with the girls when the boys were at gym, we covered the room with blinking lights and tinsel (which the girls sprinkled in their Afros, where it twinkled beautifully, like jewelry) and streamers and ornaments they had made in art class.

Then I started something new in the time after the stations. On my old tape recorder, I recorded two songs, "Up the Country" (by Canned Heat, a white country-blues group doing a song with a pastoral, flute motif), and "Stand!" (by Sly and the Family Stone, a very "funky" black group doing a rousing soul song with a message), transcribed the lyrics by stopping and starting the tape recorder, and ran off copies. At the end of a morning of stations, I had the kids pull their chairs around my desk, and I read through the two songs as poems and then played them. The impact was sensational. There was an electric connection between the printed words, the poetry, and the music. We talked about the vocabulary and the meanings of the songs, and then played them again, and Barbara looked up and said, "Dance, Mr. Marshall!"

After Christmas I recorded and wrote out the words of a number of other songs, and had the kids collate a thirty-six-page *Book of Songs*. Through the rest of the year we would listen to these in spare periods and go through the same process, and there were many stations on the lyrics and rhyme patterns of the songs. None of the subsequent sessions seemed quite as dramatic as the first one — the tape suffered from the same problem as the posters, being accepted as part of the atmosphere of the room and taken for granted — but the kids learned a great deal from the songs. We also used the tape for parties and in moments of tension (after the crisis sparked by the nurse's comments, for example). I put a lot of songs by the Beatles on the tape, and was happy to see the kids' initial disdain for "them white hippies" melt into great appreciation for some of their songs. At the beginning of the tape there was a group of twelve songs, by the Beatles, Sly, the Temptations, and Nina Simone, that they could listen to over and over again, but many of the other songs weren't as successful. I kicked myself at the end of the year for not bending more to their tastes and including more current, "bubble-gum" songs, but that was a single lost opportunity in a successful idea.

Two days before the Christmas vacation there was a lot of turmoil among the faculty about alleged plotting to oust the principal (because she was a woman), and several very tense meetings were held. Then one colleague I had been driving to the school from Cambridge announced that he was leaving the school as of the vacation and another friend said he would probably leave at the end of the year. I had a sick and helpless feeling, but could only sympathize with their feelings about staying; life was pretty stable on the sixth-grade corridor where I was, but large classes and the rising level of disruption in the school had made life impossible for them in the seventh grade. While making progress with a small number of kids seemed enough reason for me to stay around and try to change things, for them it was not enough to counterbalance the pain of every day.

There was a mood of uncertainty among my colleagues, and people stood around hoping the next day would be a snow day. But although the snow did its best, it didn't do well enough and we trickled in reluctantly the next morning to sparsely attended classes and a desultory last day. I got into a great discussion of the Kennedy assassination with a group of boys, played games, had a somewhat messy and chaotic party (the boys spat in the girls' drinks, and popcorn got scattered all over the place), and finally we all went home for ten days.

Five.

Life in Grade 6-G:

New Year's to June

I came back from vacation to find that three new people had been added to the class. Two of them, Gail and Tyrone, came from other sixth-grade classes, and I knew Tyrone because he was a friend of Freddie's and kept begging me to let him in the room before Christmas. In the middle of the morning, one of the guidance counselors came to the room with a little blue-eyed white girl from Indiana called Claire. At that point she and her brother and sister in the seventh and eighth grade were the only whites in the entire school. With kids showing these new arrivals the ropes, we all tried to get ourselves cranked up again after the vacation. Eddie had a hard time. "I feel like I'm in a sardine can," he said on Thursday, "And at the end of the day someone opens it."

At the beginning of the year when I was helping kids, I often found it hard not to tell them too much, do too much of the work for them and not let them fight through it themselves. I got this tendency under control during the fall, but had a relapse a week after returning from Christmas. I got an old manual typewriter from a friend and decided to try putting it at the Free station for kids to use when they had finished their stations. I brought it out of the closet while the girls were at gym and tried to give the boys a demonstration of how it worked; but they drove me crazy poking the keys, pushing the carriage, and pulling the levers, and finally I put it away in a huff. It was only a few minutes later that I realized how absurd this was, and I took the typewriter out and left it on a table.

Over the next few days, the typewriter was heavily used by nearly everyone in the class and people had no trouble figuring out by experimentation how it worked. Tyrone became the typewriter expert: he learned how the mechanism worked and dismantled the top regularly to clean it. He and Ralph also wrote several worksheets themselves on the typewriter and gave them out to the rest of the class. When I bought two other old manuals (for about ten dollars each), all three were in use almost every minute of the day and had a stabilizing effect on the room, especially toward the end of the station time. Some people insisted on pounding the keys as if they were playing a Tchaikovsky piano concerto, but most were extremely patient, carefully hunting-and-pecking their way through their Creative Writing or some other project, delighted at how beautiful their writing looked when they were finished.

On January 13, we got the news that Martin Luther King's birthday two days later would be a vacation for the school. The next day I brought in a recording of King's "I have a dream" speech and the transcript I had made my first year, and went over it followed by Nina Simone's superb song, "The King of Love is Dead." Both were a success, but went even better when I lent them to a colleague down the hall who was a better conventional teacher.

Later that day, a young, like-minded colleague sent me into a tailspin by suggesting that the learning stations were glorified busywork, that I was controlling my class by burying it in paperwork. Driving him home during the next few weeks, I got into one argument after another that left me distressed and uncertain about what I was doing. He insisted that we should see ourselves as guerrillas within the system, that our job was to throw little wrenches in the works, like giving a whole class A's on their report cards and trying to educate them in the things that were "really

important." I considered this self-indulgent, arguing that, having joined the system, we both had to make compromises to remain effective. But I did not feel at all comfortable making the argument and was bothered by his assertion that the stations were a way of propping up the system and deceiving the kids and their parents about what the schools were really like. I argued that giving a whole class A's (which a friend of ours actually did just before quitting in a huff the next month) only discredited any and all grades that were given and made the school rely more on standardized test scores in tracking — which didn't help anyone. Regardless of how much we despised grades and wished that they could be replaced with something more human, I argued that for the time being they were extremely important to the kids' futures. He said that we should be working to bring the system to a halt, and I felt very strange arguing that it was there to stay, would educate almost all the children in the city for the foreseeable future, and therefore had to be reformed from within, not subverted. Our differences in perspective made each of us feel that the other was irresponsible as far as the kids were concerned.

But it was his attack on the learning stations that hurt most. I wondered how you could draw a line between a stimulating decentralized classroom and a regime of worksheet repression. Surely at its best, a class of kids working individually on worksheets was far preferable to a class of passive kids listening to a teacher explain things. But it turned out that he was not contrasting my system to conventional teaching but to something much more free, a situation in which the kids made more decisions about what they were going to learn than they did in my class. I admitted that choosing the *order* in which you did the stations wasn't exactly a monumental educational decision for my kids to be making, but I argued that the responsibility of the stations was good for them and that besides, my arrangement was about as far as I felt I could go in freeing the class, considering the politics of the school.

This colleague did try to free his classes more, and his fate is significant. He was harassed more and more by the administration about the lack of "discipline" in his classes, became more and more frustrated, began to miss days of school, and finally went on a one-man strike, standing outside the school one day in March handing out leaflets condemning the conditions within the school and demanding various changes before his reinstatement. His action was received with great bitterness by the conservatives (one of whom threatened to slug him if he ever set foot in the school again), and both the principal and the liberals found him hard to defend, given the tense atmosphere of the school. In subsequent weeks there was a lot of negotiating about whether he would receive back pay and whether he might be hired by some other Boston school sometime in the future, but he had clearly burned every bridge he ever had to the King School. Those of us who remained inside the school during his solitary strike admired his guts and felt he had done many good things in the school before he had left. But he made things more difficult for us by associating many good ideas about changing the school with radical tactics, thereby discrediting them for many of our colleagues. On the other hand, we weren't doing anything very visible to reform the system in which we were working, and the prospect of major changes seemed far away. Yet we were surviving and perhaps having an effect on a small number of kids. Was that enough? My friend didn't think so. Some days we thought that perhaps it was.

But this is getting ahead of the story. Back in January my colleague's arguments got me so defensive about the stations that I moved the desks out of the groups and into short rows jutting out of the wall, with my desk in the middle of the front of the room, and tried to get more all-class activities going. I taught vigorously in this format for a couple of days, but very quickly the pressure began to build up. Putting the desks in rows had given me an opportunity to break up some of the big cliques on the girls' side of the room, but the desks were now more concentrated in one area of the room, and all the noise was projected towards the front rather than inwards into small groups. Whether by coincidence or as a result of breaking up the enclaves the kids had created for themselves, there was a rash of vicious fights on the second and third day of the new layout, and I was frustrated by the slow pace of teaching when I did it at the front.

In fact, my response to my critic's disparagement of the stations had taken me further away from what he had in mind rather than closer to it, and probably reflected other worries as well as his comments. The class moved more slowly and the kids made even fewer decisions, had even less freedom, than they had had in the stations. The kids, who had grown to appreciate the limited freedom of the stations time, were cramped in a more conventional class unless it was really exciting, and I found it hard to keep up a high level of involvement. They had not raised a single serious objection to the station system (in contrast to the early rebellion of my first year's class against my "hip" amphitheater arrangement), and now they were trying to tell me something through noise and disruption.

As the crises and confrontations mounted, I quickly recalled why I had started the stations in the first place and rediscovered their merits. Both the kids and I needed a more free-flowing setup — the problem seemed to be that we had begun to take the stations for granted and forgotten how important they were. There are teachers who can teach well in a conventional format, but my stand-up teaching was not much better than it had been the year before. Then one afternoon a friend walked into the room and said that my new arrangement of the desks looked like a bus with me in the driver's seat. That did it, and I went back to groups and stations the next morning. I decided that the kids *were* learning and the stations *were* working; it was just that there had been a string of bad days and I had been too sensitive to criticism. Clearly the class was getting very good at doing complex and challenging work, was doing a lot more of it than other classses, and was enjoying itself to boot. So I concentrated on improving my worksheets, following through more on the stations with individuals, and developing more of a sense of humor about the inevitable crises and down days and the vagaries of my colleagues.

Breaking up the string of fights that coincided with this period of instability, I felt Claire's blue eyes on me. Suddenly I, too, was twelve years old looking at myself through her disbelieving eyes. It was a very strange feeling. Once Claire came up and told me that when she had been studying for her Social Studies test she had forgotten what NAACP stood for and so had called a friend of the family's who was a friend of Huey Newton and he had told her. Then she had studied for the test for the rest of the night. Clearly she was from another planet, and the other kids showed a mixture of curiosity and hostility towards her. One afternoon she was deliberately tripped in the corridor and there was a big crisis, in which the suspicions of some of the other kids that I was being overly protective of her were confirmed. I was not surprised or heartbroken when, a little later, her mother yanked Claire and her brother and sister out of the King School.

There was always a lot in the way of conversation, kids acting out songs, and other small dramas going on during the station time. At the beginning of February I got the idea of putting some of these actors on the stage and letting the whole class watch them perform, because some of them were very good. But when I tried this, there was only one person who was brave enough to perform — Freddie. He did a superb imitation of a drunkard and delighted the rest of the kids, but no one else would stand up in front of the whole class. I was amazed, and rediscovered yet another advantage of the stations — they provided a number of *smaller* stages on which less brazen kids could perform for smaller audiences of friends and gradually build up their confidence. A while later I walked into a very strict conventional class down the hall and knew how my kids felt when I asked them to perform for the whole class: this class was so quiet, and the attention of the kids was so focused on the front of the room, that I actually got stage fright walking in and handing a piece of paper to the teacher. I remembered this kind of classroom from my own schooling and how it had inhibited the development of my own powers of expression and confidence, how it nurtured the habit of sitting back and watching other people make fools of themselves and not stepping forward yourself. During the year the many small stages of the station time brought several very shy kids out of their shells and gave everyone an opportunity for self-expression without fear of ridicule.

The day before the February vacation was a rather unusual one. A city-wide black high-school students' boycott was in progress, and there was a lot of talk that the King students would have a walkout in sympathy with them. The atmosphere was tense as the entire school filed into the auditorium for a film and lecture on dental health, and it seemed a guaranteed bust. But when the projector was turned on, the auditorium was as silent as it had been in a long time. The reason: a gorgeous black girl was the subject of the film's injunctions to brush right and see a dentist regularly and prevent cavities, and the entire student body gazed on her longingly for half an hour.

Then, after lunch, there was a walkout of sorts, but it was more like a carnival. The administration took the very sensible attitude that if the kids wanted to leave, it wasn't going to try to stop them, but most of the kids stayed in the school, milling around the corridors and happily socializing with each other, and occasionally explaining to an incredulous teacher just what it was they were protesting.

When we returned from the winter vacation, Eddie said that he wished he were dead so that he wouldn't have to come to school any more. Nevertheless, things were going well. Over the vacation I had visited a few public schools in Princeton, and now I watched my own class with the eyes of an observer. I was impressed by the kids' independence, the way they ran around getting the work and helping each other, and at this point I began to recover fully from the period of uncertainty that had plagued me during the winter.

The next day I arranged a visit by a black Olympic ath-

lete who worked in the school, and we spent the period before he came cooking up a stream of questions to ask him and wrote them on the board. When he arrived, the kids were delighted and impressed. He talked about the Olympics in Mexico City, his own development, and managed to make some allusions to the problems of the school. Once, he said, he had been ahead in a race and still had lost because he hadn't had enough confidence in himself. He then turned to Larry and said that *he* didn't either, judging from the way he acted around the school. Larry got the message.

At the end of the day, when the girls had left for Music, George grappled with a smaller boy and I roughly tore him off. At this, George completely lost his temper and threw a chair at me. I fended it off, sent the rest of the boys off to Music, and then shouted at him that he might very well have two assault charges against him, one from the boy's parents and one from me. That subdued him a little, but he collected himself and said that he had been meaning to have a talk with me for a long time about the way I was running the class, although now it was too late since he and his family were about to leave Boston. Surprised, I told him to say what he had to say anyway, and he replied that I was not mean enough, that I should have clamped down on Calvin and Freddie and him when they talked back to me and swore — that I should have suspended them and punished them more than I had. But now since I hadn't been tough at the beginning they laughed at me when I got mad and didn't do their work. He said that if I had a real talk with the class, I would find that most everyone else felt the same way about me that he did, although they didn't want to come right out and say it. He said that the way I got the class together was no way at all, and I didn't get down to any *real* teaching.

Feeling a great deal more confident than I had a month before, and recognizing every word of his arguments from previous arguments with other teachers, I retorted that I thought the learning stations were a better form of teaching and were working fine except for a few boys, himself included, who were going through a bad spell. I asked him whether there weren't more kids doing nothing in most other classes he had been in, and he admitted that there were. Besides, I continued, I was not a mean person inside and couldn't function that way, so if I tried to act "bad" as he suggested, it wouldn't be real and people would know it right away. He agreed with this too. Then I launched into a thing about how I hadn't come to the King School to shout at kids or get them in trouble but to help them learn, and I said I thought most of them were learning in our class most of the time.

I asked him what he thought I could do to improve the situation for kids like him who were turned off, to get them more involved in the work. He replied somewhat scornfully that it was really too late and about all I could do for the rest of the year was to keep bringing in interesting work — which from George seemed the supreme compliment. Then I asked him what he thought I should do about his throwing the chair at me, whether, according to his ideas of how I should act, I should take him to the office and report him. But he said no, I should give him another chance. I smiled and marched him to the office and wrote a report on what had happened. But he had the last laugh; he left the school for good that afternoon, and once again escaped the punishment that part of him sought so successfully to avoid and part of him thought he so richly deserved. I never saw him again.

The beginning of March found me in a momentary depression. The previous Saturday I'd had a field trip with a group of boys that they loved but which had left my eardrums beaten in and my body exhausted. We sledded down part of Blue Hill on sheets of plywood, played touch football (when I snarled the signals Joe Namath style, Freddie was so delighted that he rolled around on the ground and kept imitating me for the rest of the year), and ate fried chicken in the car when it rained. There was a lot of calling me "college boy" and a few boys tried unsuccessfully to get a rise out of me by calling me Kim. The next Monday I was still tired, and in the back of my mind was a slight worry about an older boy who had threatened grimly that he was coming up to get me with a gun that day. There was a period after the stations when I didn't have anything planned and people wandered aimlessly around the room making a lot of noise. I got very uptight that someone might walk in and demand to know what was going on. Then I got the news that a young, like-minded colleague had been fired as of the end of the year for not being able to "control" his classes, and my depression was deepened.

A couple of days later the problem of my class's behavior in the corridors on the way to other parts of the school came to a head. I had not taken the business of "filing" (marching down the right side of the corridor "quickly and quietly") very seriously, and my class often looked more like a demonstration than a line of well-behaved schoolchildren. I got a lot of static from an administrator, and even more when we had a few false fire alarms and my girls ran around having fun outside instead of standing in line. I decided that I was at my worst telling them to do something that I didn't believe in myself, and I was uncomfortable and resentful in this role. There was just no way I could make the kids think that "filing" was of the slightest importance to their education, but I was constantly embarrassed by other teachers berating the kids and stepping in to "control" them better.

Throughout March and April there was a rash of false fire alarms, sometimes four or five a day, and a number of fights between Freddie and Ralph, most of them stemming from welfare and mother insults. Again and again, the bells would bong and we would heave sighs and walk out of the building; and I would wade into the fights and have to get Freddie in an arm-lock to keep him from hurting Ralph who, although half his size, remained defiant, struggling to carve out his manhood. Very close to the end of the year, Ralph succeeded. He got into a real fight with a boy more his own size, and when I broke it up there was general agreement among the boys that he had been on top.

From then on he had a "bad" reputation and was much more well-respected.

The girls helped a lot to get me through this period. On the eleventh of March, while the boys were down at gym, they had a colleague lure me out of the room for a few minutes and then sent someone down to call me back to "break up a fight." The room was darkened, and they all jumped up and screamed "Happy Birthday!" and turned on the lights. The room was all rearranged with the floor swept and Cokes and potato chips and napkins on the desks, and one blackboard was covered with some ego-boosting inscriptions. But when the boys came back, they were furious that they hadn't been in on the party, and gave me a hard time for the rest of the day.

A few days later I picked up an old carpet from the attic of my mother's house and spread it across the middle of the room in the station time. People were at first bewildered by it. Visitors typically asked me what on earth it was doing there, and the janitors kicked and cursed it. At first a few girls lay down on it to read, but found that the boys were looking up their dresses and gave up the idea. The boys saw it as a boxing and wrestling ring and gravitated to it with their disputes and horseplay; unfortunately I wasn't relaxed enough to let them do this or take off my glasses and join them. So the rug just sat there for the rest of the year, softening the atmosphere of the room a little. ("It makes it more homey," I would explain to the incredulous visitors), and deadening the fierce acoustics of the room by a few degrees. With this new element in the room, the kids rearranged their desks and groups for the umpteenth time.

Throughout the winter and spring, Freddie was a major problem. He stopped bothering the girls, but seemed unable to concentrate on his work for more than a few seconds. We liked each other, and he claimed on numerous occasions that I was the best teacher he had ever had, but he was constantly in trouble, and I was under heavy pressure from other kids and teachers to punish him conventionally. Every once in a while I would succumb for lack of anything better to do, but it didn't do any good. The frustrating thing was that he could do the work well, but he only finished his stations when I spent a great deal of time with him or kept him after school and worked with him alone.

During the spring he got into trouble with a number of older kids by picking on people who had big, "bad" eighth-grade brothers, cousins, and boy friends, and most of the rest of the year he was being pursued by three separate people, each one ready to beat the living daylights out of him. When the heat was really on, he didn't dare go to the cafeteria for lunch, and lurked around the corridors hiding behind people or pulling his head down inside his jacket. I had to rescue him a few times, and maybe this was the reason he stuck around me so much. Or was it the other way around? Did he provoke these older kids in order to attract more attention from me so that I would have to save his skin and he would have to stick around me?

Whenever I sat down with Freddie and tried to talk about what he was doing to other people and to himself, we didn't seem to get anywhere. He would say that the reason he was acting so bad was that I didn't like him anymore, and I would say that I liked him fine but didn't like some of the crazy things he was doing, particularly hurting other people. But I don't think he got the distinction I was trying to draw between him and his actions. Toward the end of the year I tried a different tack: if he liked me, why did he act so badly in my class when he acted better for other, more authoritarian, teachers he didn't like? The only conclusion I could draw from this, I said, was that he didn't like me and had no respect for me. This made him think and was a little more effective, but not much. It may also have given him the idea of acting up more with these other teachers to even the score.

The girls were resentful that I was so friendly with such a "bad" kid, and were constantly after me to take a more hard line on Freddie and a group of other boys that occasionally chased them after school. But during the spring I got more and more friendly with this group of boys (Freddie, Tyrone, Calvin, Eddie, and Larry) and was hard pressed to take their bad behavior very seriously. This group was often waiting for me when I came to school three quarters of an hour early in the morning, and after school we would go outside and horse around if the weather was fine.

One day when we were outside after school, my glasses got knocked off. I caught them and looked up to find that the boys had all taken a step back and were scrutinizing the new and unfamiliar face (they had been begging me to take them off for weeks). After a pause they decided that they liked it better without the glasses, although it took some getting used to. "Look at that profile!" said Eddie. "Get that nose!" They got so excited on this and other occasions that the doorman and I had to slam the school door in their faces to get them to go home. For a while their favorite pastime was repeating an epithet I was meant to have uttered when a taxi driver cut in front of us in traffic on one of the field trips. They often did this in front of other teachers, much to my embarrassment. Sometimes they would slip out of other classes they were bored with and try to get me to chase them, and a few times I obliged (although this didn't impress the teachers of these classes very much).

To me, the whole relationship with these boys was full of affection, but some other teachers saw it as a clear case of kids running all over a weak, liberal teacher for whom they had no respect. I tried to explain to the boys that there were times and places when we should be "cool" with one another because of these unsympathetic people. But they never seemed to understand this, and there were a few times when I felt obliged to be unpleasant with them in public for appearance's sake.

Despite misgivings about my way of handling the boys, there was a group of girls that was almost equally close to me, though our relationship was much more coy. At the end of the tearful crisis about

the nurse's comments, there was a stirring among them and Mona said, "Mr. Marshall, we're sorry." I was touched and said, "You'd better watch out — I might start crying again," to which Valerie said, "Let's get out of here. I don't want to get flooded!"

More of the girls' appreciation of me and the class reached me through the stations. Helen would occasionally write the praises of the system on one of them, and another girl wrote on her Creative Writing one day, "I want to run to school every day to learn more than I am doing now. Because I don't do nothing at home but sit in the house till next day for school." And there were a series of inscriptions on the walls and blackboards during the spring: "Sexy dexy Marshall," "You been a good teacher," "We all hate you," and "Mr. Marshall is a good guy."

Even when they pouted, some of the girls could be charming. Alice had the lock stolen from her locker door, and was furious that I couldn't do anything about it. For the entire morning she screeched, "I want my lock!" and when I succeeded in ignoring her, she handed in her stations with "I want my lock!" written on every single line. And when I broke up a fight between Sheila and a boy, her imitation-leather coat got a massive tear in the armpit, and she announced, "You're going to sew that up, Mr. Marshall!" There were other girls who were jealous of the attention these girls got from me and less enthusiastic about the class. One day we returned from lunch to find that two filing cabinet drawers filled with old station sheets had been emptied onto the floor and a couple of posters ripped from the walls. It was not as bad as a similar incident the year before, but I was distressed when I got a report (never confirmed because of another crisis that afternoon) that it had been done by some girls in our class.

The girls as a group also had a capacity for real cruelty to one another. This only emerged once in the year, when all of them suddenly decided that Sarah's skirts were too short and too alluring to the boys. The razzing she got was brutal. ("She's crying because she knows what we're saying is *true!*" exclaimed one of her tormentors in the middle.) The business lasted for

ten screeching minutes despite my attempts to intervene and assert her right to wear what she pleased.
Finally some of the girls went over to her side and
defended her, and it subsided. I was left with an abid-
ing respect for Sarah's guts in sticking out the attack.
I thought of some of the boys who would have run
out of the room in hysterics at the very beginning.

At the end of March I felt another crisis had come in
the stations, and I divided the class into three large
groups, which meant consolidating a number of
smaller groups. I asked each group to elect officers
and decide on a number of rules for themselves which
they themselves would enforce. For a while this was
effective, and the reshuffling shook loose a few
friendships that had been fading and formed new and
fresher alliances. But I didn't follow through with this
idea by treating the groups as groups consistently —
taking them on trips together, dismissing them together, having them collect money for various projects (although I later discovered that one of the girls'
groups had done just this on its own), or having them
correct their own work. The shift had only a marginal
effect on the room, and I later decided that I had
been crisis-hungry.

Scattered through the year were days when absolutely everything seemed to go wrong. March 24 was
one of those days. A couple of boys romped around
the room sparring with each other all morning and
refused to pay any attention to me. The girls were
flirting with some seventh-graders who were watching the fire box in the corridor outside the class, and,
to get a better view, ripped apart a new National
Geographic chart on pollution which was taped to the
door. Alice screeched at me about something, and
in the middle of lunch a false fire alarm sounded (despite the guards throughout the building) and caused
complete confusion. In the afternoon someone's locker
was broken into and she was in tears and furious
at me because I couldn't do anything. After a terribly
chaotic trip to Music, another fire alarm sounded and
we were out in the cold again. As I was breaking up

a small fight on the embankment outside, I smelled burning fabric and whirled around too late to stop someone who had just come up behind me with a cigarette and burned two holes in the pants of my new corduroy suit.

All over the school there was a feeling of looseness and chaos, and an older black teacher was set upon by a group of eighth-grade girls. Several very level-headed teachers suggested that the school be closed down for a few days to give us a chance to get ourselves together and think of some more effective programs before the school exploded. (It seems that violence or the threat of violence had been the main impetus for reform or thoughts of reform in the school. All the changes of two years before hadn't changed that.)

The school was not closed. But days like this one had a way of being followed by days that were remarkably placid. Perhaps having survived the worst gave us a one-day ticket to respect and affection — or perhaps the kids were just resting. Certainly there had been no solution of the problems that were steadily building up the pressure within the school, which led some of us to conclude that the future was very much in the hands of the kids, that the school operated at their will.

A few afternoons later I had an exceptionally warm time with Eddie, Calvin, and Larry after school. We laughed a lot, and I finally drove them home. A few days later, in a similar after-school session, Eddie got the storyteller's gleam in his eye and spent ten minutes telling us all the story of the one time in his school career that he had been suspended. He had been scared and provoked by a teacher and had pulled a knife on him. He told the story with finesse and perspective, capturing his own predicament standing in a corner holding an illegal knife; the teacher, uptight, embarrassed, trying to get it away from him; and the principal fretting around in the wings, not knowing *what* to do.

Despite these moments, I was conscious of being

taken for granted by many of the other kids at this point in the year, and was rather relieved when, coming into the class twenty minutes late a few days after this, I was greeted by dead silence and a morning of angelic behavior. At first I was confused, but then realized that the kids had realized from my absence what a difference my presence made. This made me think that perhaps I should take a day off from time to time to make them pay more attention to me, but that seemed a little self-indulgent. After all, it was probably better for them to be working hard, not constantly aware of the presence of a teacher in the room.

In the middle of April, I had a demonstration of the effect that the independent activity of the stations was having on the kids. I came into school after wasting the previous evening watching a movie on television. I had done absolutely no preparation — no stations, nothing. Before school I scrambled around and got enough copies of *Scope* magazine for the class, and plopped them down in front of everyone when they came in. Luckily the issue had a play in it, and I thought we might be able to read it as a class although we hadn't had very good luck doing this before. But before I could begin, two groups of girls assigned parts among themselves and started reading the play on their own. The boys read it with me, and a few people not involved in the groups sat around and did the crossword and word games in the magazine and took old tests on which they wanted to improve their standing on the charts. This went on for the entire day, and I was in seventh heaven. But I realized that it was partly a lucky combination of moods, and I wasn't ready to embark on an "open classroom" yet. I came in the next morning with a full load of stations. Another significant thing happened on this day of play-reading. Several boys got involved in reading with the girls' groups, and although there was still some tittering and foolishness, I was pleased to see the rare display of peaceful coexistence between the sexes in the class. These small, tentative contacts increased for the remainder of the year, but were never more than that.

In April, there were two incidents in the cafeteria. I broke up a fight by pulling one of the kids out of it by the foot. Later, I chased a boy out of the cafeteria who had stolen Larry's hat, retrieved the hat, and turned around to find a hundred boys spilling out of the cafeteria to see the action. A moment later someone came up to me and said, "You're crazy, Mr. Marshall." It was a compliment.

Outside the school that afternoon, I noticed a group of girls picking on a bespectacled, intellectual child in 6-A who you could guarantee would have a hard time in almost any school. One of her tormentors claimed angrily that this girl had kicked her jumprope during gym class, and so was going to "get her behind kicked." Her friends encouraged her and whopped the girl on the back of the head when she was looking the other way and scattered her books all over the sidewalk. Not that it would change the behavior of the bullies or make things any easier for the girl in the future, I nevertheless intervened and escorted the victim down the street. But the other girls followed and the leader ran up full tilt from behind and pushed the girl, glasses flying, knees scraping, flat on her face. I whirled around but it was too late to do anything at all; I had a sick, helpless feeling as I took the weeping girl back to the school for a more efficient escort home. Still, the girl was back in school the next day, tougher and more ready for this kind of treatment and more savvy in avoiding it.

At the beginning of May I had a new idea for the Social Studies station. I cut out the pictures from a long *Life* magazine spread on the events of the sixties and glued them onto four sheets of colored cardboard. I then wrote a long worksheet (which spilled over into the General station) asking questions about the pictures and captions, and stuck the cardboard sheets onto a blackboard. During the morning people came up in twos and threes and answered the questions. It was never too crowded and everyone got a close look at the pictures and enjoyed them, although they couldn't figure out why that decade

had been such a disastrous one for the country. Before the end of the year I used this same technique with some *Life* pictures of China and the inside of the human body, and put up a series of prints of famous paintings for similar treatment in the Creative Writing station. All of these projects were conducive to being followed up by some kind of all-class discussion when people had finished working through the questions alone, and I got a lot of mileage out of each one.

From this point to the end of the year, Steven began to work like crazy, and I still don't know what brought about the breakthrough. Where he had turned his head away from Math in frustration for eight months, he suddenly concentrated, let me help him more, and volunteered to stay after school to work on taking old tests again. By the end of the year he had passed nearly all the Math units on the chart, and took home a straight A on his report card and a clean manila folder of his A and A+ papers for the last two months.

In the middle of May Freddie returned from his umpteenth suspension and on his first day back in school threw a freshly chewed, wet piece of bubble gum into his Reading teacher's hair. (He maintained, and probably firmly believed, that it had "slipped" out of his hand.) She had to cut a whole lock of hair to get it out, and we agreed that whatever we were doing with Freddie, it wasn't working. I wondered whether I should have him transferred to a more authoritarian class, and at this point seriously considered it, especially since a lot of his behavior around the school was being blamed on me. But when I thought about it some more, I decided that this would only put a lid on the things that were going on in his head and build up the pressure even more. I felt that a more open setting had to be better for him, even though I wasn't getting very far with him except making him a little happier. Perhaps if I had him for another year I would start to get somewhere, but at the moment this is impossible.

May 12 was another one of those days. At 8:45 in the morning we had the first false alarm of the day, and when the kids were outside some of the eighth-graders discovered the naked mutilated dead body of a white woman in a vacant lot next to the school. During the rest of the day there were five more false alarms, and whatever was going on in the room was completely discombobulated. The alarms were perfectly designed to disrupt the school: they exhausted teachers more than kids, and gave one person with a chip on his shoulder the power to turn out the entire building. Furthermore, they violated the insularity that I had been striving to establish in our room. But I did feel that the stations were disrupted less by the alarms than were more conventionally taught classes, since kids could return and pick up where they had left off instead of spending ten minutes getting settled down to complete silence for a teacher-run class. After this day, the school made a more concerted effort to stop the alarms by posting teachers, aides, and students under all the boxes around the school all the time, but some were still rung nearly every day.

A few days later we went on a school field trip to the Wonder Bread bakery in the suburbs. The kids were excited as we got on the buses, although Freddie got yanked off when he yelled, "You jerk!" at me. We had a successful trip, and as we drove along Blue Hill Avenue on the way back, we passed a place where I had brought a group of girls on a field trip in the fall. I turned to Helen and asked her whether she remembered coming out here. For some reason there was a lull of conversation in the bus at that moment, and everyone heard the question and looked out of the window of the bus. We had passed the spot, and all they saw was thick, inviting forest. It took a while to live that down.

A few days later, afflicted by bronchitis, I managed to get through the entire day without speaking a single word. I wrote the kids a little letter in the morning explaining the situation, and after they had satisfied themselves that I was not putting them on, they did very well. Perhaps this wouldn't have worked out as well in a class more dependent on the teacher's vocal cords.

That same weekend Sam, who had been drumming and singing and dancing his way around the room for the entire year, brought down the house in a neighborhood concert and came into school on Monday standing about a foot taller. We had gone through a period of deep alienation, and our relationship never really recovered from one time when I insulted him in a moment of anger earlier in the year. But at this point he had put himself on the map.

As the year drew to a close, I also realized that I had not done nearly enough for Larry, whom I had promised myself not to lose at the very beginning of the year. He went on trips and got lots of attention, but somehow it wasn't enough, and he would poke and pester me a lot. After a day of this at the end of May, I lost patience and socked him in the stomach, not hard, but enough to make the point. The next morning he came in early and announced that his mother and brother were coming up to the school to take me to court for assault. When Tyrone corroborated the story, I got worried and blew my cool, and it wasn't until fifteen minutes later that I found out that they were putting me on. Larry reveled in my embarrassment; perhaps this was what he had been looking for — a little weakness in me, a victory for himself. Or perhaps it was that he had heard that he wouldn't be at the school the next year because his family was moving to another part of the city, and wanted to say something else to me.

In the first week of June I took the boys on a swimming trip, and two weeks later took eleven of the girls; both trips were successful, a fitting culmination of the trips of the year. As I drove the girls back into Roxbury in a borrowed VW bus, there was a lot of eager chatter and cute little things like, "Oh Mr. Marshall, you're so sweet to take us to the beach tomorrow." Then the radio came on with "Want Ad," a great favorite, and within two bars the entire crew had picked it up and was singing it in tune, word-perfect, right to the end, like a sweet traveling choir.

From March on, the school had no pencils because we had used up our quota, and I had to buy my own. This led to innumerable hassles as kids came up asking for their third pencil of the day. Every time I found myself getting angry at someone for losing pencils, I stepped back and realized how absurd it was and went out and bought some more. The basic problem was a widespread hoarding instinct among the kids that stemmed from years of skimping on materials by schools. Perhaps an atmosphere of continuing generosity and abundance by a teacher or a school would break this psychology and result in a net saving of materials.

The last weeks of school were hard. From the seventh-grade corridor there were tales of minor riots and fights between students and teachers, and we walked to the parking lot through a sea of paper, chairs, desks, paint trays, and strips of metal that had been heaved out of the third-floor windows of a couple of classes that for various reasons were unattended some of the time. Then there was a major fire in one of the boys' bathrooms, and for once the alarm bells meant business. Morale among the teachers sank even lower with the news that another 200 students would arrive at the school the next year, bringing the enrollment close to 1,000, and the faculty would be cut by one-third as part of a city-wide austerity program. Although both of these predictions turned out to be exaggerated, there was no program, no reason to believe that the gradually escalating pressure would do anything but keep building.

June 15 was another one of those days. After an amazingly placid morning, there was a rash of fights in the room. I broke up a particularly vicious one in the corridor that was being cheered on by a crowd of 75 kids, and nearly got bitten by one of the pugilists (a few minutes later a colleague pointed out a tuft of black hair caught behind one of my shirt buttons). Then I heard about a series of fights between Helen and Anne, who were competing with each other to become the most spectacular and well-behaved students in the class. But the day ended well. Somehow the families of both girls came up to the school that afternoon, and for the only time in the entire year we talked out the problem to absolutely everyone's satisfaction. Still, both girls were suspended for three days by the administration and the room wasn't the same until they returned.

In the last week of school, Freddie had some more bad luck. Fighting with Alice, he got bitten on the arm so hard it drew blood. And the next day he slugged her in retaliation and broke two of his own fingers.

That afternoon I had to give out the report cards and tell kids what section they were going to be promoted to in the seventh grade (no one was kept back). I was pleased that nine people in the class were being boosted into "academic" sections and was sure that this would greatly improve their chances in the future. But I got more and more angry at the system of tracking when I heard kids talking about how so-and-so was going into a "smart" class and so-and-so was going into a "dumb" class, and X was better than Y because she was going into 7-E while he was in 7-F.

The effect of the tracking system on the kids was perhaps the most deeply disruptive element of the school year. I delivered a long lecture on how it was only the difference between "academic" and "nonacademic" sections that made a difference, and even this did not mean anything in terms of many other abilities and talents; but I don't expect that what I said had much impact on them because the letters still stand there and they know the order of the alphabet.

In the course of the year, one of the major jobs I had, along with the other teachers of "general" sections, was giving the kids more confidence in themselves than they were given by this invidious system. Like

any meritocratic system, it gave to some (I had several opportunities to observe the comparative stability and self-esteem of the "academic" classes) and took away from many.

The last day of school was a culmination of many things. I started off by giving the kids a sixty-question series of sheets asking them about the stations and the year. The results were gratifying. In questionnaires I had done before Christmas, the kids consistently said that they liked the stations, but that I was not *mean* enough and there was too much noise in the room. We worked on these problems during the year — that is, we tried to lower the noise and I tried to convince them that a teacher doesn't have to be mean to be good — and I found that in this final questionnaire most of them had completely turned around on both issues. They had gotten used to the level of noise and to my quiet, oblique, and individualized style of teaching and discipline and no longer insisted on my being a tough guy all the time. In the questionnaire, all but one of the kids said they preferred stations to conventional classes. Most thought they had worked harder than in other classes, preferred station worksheets to textbooks, and thought I gave them enough help and more attention than other teachers. All but one said they had learned a lot ("alot, alot, alot" wrote Vickey), and most thought there had been fewer fights in our room than in others in which they had been. Most people thought they had learned to write better and had become more competent in the basics of Math and English. Almost everyone admitted that "a little" copying had gone on during the station time, but denied that it was serious. On the question of my "meanness," seven kids still thought I was "not mean enough," fifteen thought I was "about right," and none that I was "too mean."

The negative comments had to do with my admitted laxity in giving and collecting homework, the fact that I didn't always make one girl do all her work, and the fact that we didn't have stations every day of the week.

Here is Helen's final comment:

I think stations are good for kids to do. Because they learn more. And they are better than the way other teachers teach and you understand things more than in regular class. And I work harder than I ever had when I do the stations. But the harder the better for me. And I have learned a lot by stations and I think other kids have too. And I enjoy school now with stations because school seems better than before with stations. And it is a fun thing to do.

I would change the desks around. And I would let the class be less noisy. And I would bring games and stuff to school when they are through with their work. And I would let the kids do Spelling every other week and I would learn them more about blacks and slavery.

And I hope your next year class would make you feel good by liking the stations like we did. Mr. Marshall if your next year class do not like the stations still give them to them. Because later on in the year they will feel different about it like we did.

When they had finished answering the questions (which they did in dead silence for half an hour), I went through the list of the class, reading a brief citation on each kid, a list of the things that had made each person special during the year, and then gave everyone an eight-by-ten black-and-white picture of himself which I had taken in the final weeks of school. Then we eased into a quiet and relaxed party, playing records and eating potato chips and talking to each other.

In a few minutes the year was over.

Six.

If I Was an Elephant
I Would Be the King:
Creative Writing from Grade 6-G

The Creative Writing station was the most uneven of all the stations. Some days kids would pour out their most intimate thoughts, but most of the time it took a lot of coaxing by me to get most people to write a few reluctant lines on the topic I suggested. Some people, like Helen and Lucy, consistently wrote a full page a day, while others never wrote anything.

I never graded the Creative Writing or tampered with spelling and grammar. Instead, I wrote a general comment at the end and hoped that the lessons learned in the English and Spelling stations would filter through to the Creative Writing station during the year. In most cases this did happen, but I was disappointed in the writing after Christmas and decided that there wasn't enough structure to it. I decided that the next year I would make a length requirement, a full page every two days, to get people writing more.

Here are some examples of 6-G's writing. The great majority of it was done before Christmas while the novelty of the station was still a strong factor.

I had a best friend. Every day we went to school together and were in the same room and rode the bus together. When we came home I had to change clothes and I went over to his house and sometimes he came over to mine. Every morning he picked me up for school and then we went to school and had fun all day. And from then on we were friends. Then school was out. He went swimming and got caught under the net and drowned and had a funeral. And his name was Kenneth.

———

Well I think a best friend should be white or black and should care what happens to you and should share things together. I have a friend like that. And she is very nice and pretty. When we go to lunch she always sits beside me and shares her snacks with me, and when she does not have any lunch I share mine with her. We are both like each other.

———

I have a friend called Angel. She is my best friend. She's like a sister to me and I am like a sister to her. And we wear each others' clothes and shoes and earrings and other things. We share things and when one of us does not have what the other one has we cut it in half and share it. And we never have a fight. That is what a good friend is and I can always count on her when I need her. And she can always count on me. So she's happy and I'm happy so we both are happy. And I'm glad.

———

Once upon a time I was awakened by my friend. Somebody died. So we all went and when everybody came in the house broke down. My mother was there and she was the only one who escaped. The rest were all wet with hot water.

———

Once upon a time in the nineteenth century I was laying down just about to go to sleep when I heard a foot step. Thump, thump, thump and I looked up and saw Frankinstein and died.

———

One day there was a storm and all the lights went out and it was dark and no one was home but me. There were no candles in the house so I turned on the switch for the lights. They came on for a little while, then went off again and I got scared again. And then my mother came home.

———

One day I was walking down the forest and all of a sudden I got tired so I lay down and when I awoke I saw a witch house with bats and animals and monsters so I was so frightened that I ran and ran and ran and all of a sudden I was in the beautiful forest and I was getting up from the ground. Then I knew I had a bad dream so I was happy again and never leave the house without my mother's permission.

––––––––

I was sad when I saw a dog get hit by a car and the man just kept going and didn't stop to see if the dog is all right.

––––––––

The day I was happy was a Saturday when we went to New York and that was the first time I was out of town. We went to a farm and we took pictures. We went to Connecticut and we stopped at Howard Johnson.

––––––––

The day I get my bicycle is when I am happy. When I get hurt is when I am sad.

––––––––

When I am mad I don't want anybody to jump on my back because I will off them. I do not play because it might be serious. When I am happy I let it all hang out: the old saying, Smile and the world will smile with you.

––––––––

Sometimes I have been sad about not being able to ride my bicycle and I was sad because my brother always gets the money and I never get any money. And I've been sad I could not ride go-carts.

––––––––

I am always happy when my brother's girlfriend comes over and she always gives me money. And I am happy when my birthday comes. I am always sad when I have to get up in the morning to go to school.

––––––––

It was a warm summer day and my big sister was going to Los Angeles for her vacation. I thought she was bringing me with her so I was glad, but when she was leaving and I saw she didn't let me go with her I was very sad. Then in the evening I heard the door-bell ring and I went down and opened the door and there she was. When she told me she came back for me I was very happy and I went with her.

––––––––

The only time I am happy is when I don't have to do work in the house. And the only time I am sad is in school and when I am home. I am glad when I am riding my bike. And some time I don't finish my work so my mother says to me you are not going outside until you finish your work and I am mad.

———

One day my friend was playing in the playground and we were on the monkey bars and some teenage boys came in the playground and then one of the boys took out a razor and they started playing games with it, and then they were playing for a while. Then suddenly one of them lost the knife and they left so my friend David went to swing and then David saw the knife and got off the swing and picked it up, and then he started playing catch with it. He played catch for a while, then he threw it up high, and I told him not to catch it but he did, and it went right through the palm of his hand and I took him home and his older sister took him to the hospital and I felt sad I was left alone.

———

I would like to be 13 and when I am 13 I want to be 14 and I'll keep going on up higher in age until I get to be 21, and when I'm 21 I'll bet you I wish I was 13 again.

———

When I get big I want to be a secretary. I would like to help my mother do her work and send my brother and sister to school every day and when my mother goes to work I clean the house and when she comes the house is clean.

———

I would like to go all around Boston for a summer and have a lot of prizes and have more things. And I want to go to Hawaii for a year and go to New York for a year and go all around the place for a summer.

———

I would like someday to have somebody who I can tell all my thoughts. In any thing I am doing I would like to tell that person, and that person can help me do everything I am doing. Going somewhere I would like that person to come with me and that person can make me happy when I am lonely. And I would like to do these same things for that person too. I really wish I could meet someone like that.

———

Dear Mr. Nixon,

I am going to talk about drugs today and how to prevent *dope* from young and old people. One way is to have all your policemen and women to go around turning houses upside down looking for pills and stuff and if they need any pills to lose weight, to gain weight, or to get better from sickness give them *shots*.

Dear Mr. Nixon,

I wish you could try to stop the bad pollution and stop the bad schools and try to stop the drugs people use these days. I hope you can because some people die from them and they don't care, they think it is good but they don't know that it isn't doing anything but hurting them.

Dear Mr. Nixon,

We need better schools and houses and churches. Someone needs to stop air pollution. Take cars out and bring horses back in. Help the people over in Biafra. Send them food, money, clothing and care. You should be ashamed of yourself.

Dear Mr. Nixon,

I think you should do something about people killing each other in the streets. The war in Vietnam, I think you should do something to stop the war and get people to stop fighting. And if you can stop these things, America should have peace and freedom. Let people know what they should not do. And I think when this is stopped, America would be a better place.

Dear Mr. Nixon,

You should stop the war in Vietnam and make a better school and better and brighter lights and paint the rooms different colors and stop the smuggling of drugs and then they cannot buy any drugs and the head man cannot sell it.

Dear Mr. Nixon,

How are you? Fine I hope. I am very happy to write to you. I wanted to do this a long time ago and now I have the chance. I think in Vietnam it's a crime for those men to fight the way they fight. Why can't there be peace? I know some white people do not like blacks and some blacks do not like whites, but I am black and I still like whites and I have lots of white friends. And I live in a ghetto and there are nice teachers that come to black neighborhoods and teach at black schools. And I think that's very nice of them because some whites are scared to come in the black neighborhood. And some blacks are scared to come in white neighborhood because of their race.

———

I go to the King School. It is a nice school. But the children in it got to go. I have a nice teacher but he seems mean because the children make him mean. And a boy named Freddie is out of sight. And on Monday we have gym. I have a friend named Helen and she is nice and cute. And for food we have hot dogs and tuna fish. And for dessert we have cake and Jell-O.

———

I go to the King School right across the street from my house. I go to gym Monday and Wednesday and we have fun. The kids are nice but bad. I have friends that I met here and old friends that I already knew. I just hate those teachers always making noise. They talk talk talk more than we do. But lunch time is my best time because I like the food, but the beans gotta go. And my friends hate those beans too. And we really get mad when we can't have cake when it is our time to get up. They always say the rest is for the second lunch. And some of the food we have is: tuna, fish, hot dog, cake, Jell-O.

———

I've been angry because when I had to go to the store five times because:
1. I forgot the money
2. I forgot what to get
3. I went to my friend's house and lost the money outside and had to get some more money.
4. I forgot what to get again because I was playing around
5. I got a beating for not obeying.
That is when I got mad and angry and the next time I went to the store I remembered every thing that time.

———

When you feel happy and glad and everybody is your

friend now. Feel proud of yourself when you're up and around.

_____

Like if it was dark and night and you were going someplace the next day then you would try to go to sleep but you can't. Later you fall to sleep and it will be morning. Then you will jump up and get ready.

_____

You feel happy and you can really do your thing!!!

_____

I had a dream
that I was a gangster
and I robbed banks
and robbed trains
and had good friends
who were gangsters.

_____

I had a dream. I was 13 years old and I was working as a nurse. I used to dress people and give them health and they may be able to read, write, talk and walk.

_____

I had a dream that I saw a man that looked just like my father. We all were in the parlor and my father was in the chair watching T.V. and my mother told me to get her some water. See my room is right off the parlor so I had to go through the room to go in the kitchen so I was near the parlor door and I saw that man that I said that looked like my father sitting on the bed.

_____

I had a dream about a bicycle and I was riding it. I went up and down the street. And I have always wanted a bike. But did not get one. My mother said that she was going to get me one. And then she said that she was not going to get me one. Because people have been hurting kids that have bikes. Then she said that if she gets a bike it would have to be both of ours.

_____

Every day I see cars going by my street and dogs and cats, boys and girls, men and ladies. I hear airplanes going by and I hear little children playing, some riding bikes, some running, and when teenagers pass by, the girls, I smell perfume on them and it smells good. And sometimes I be looking at boys race on their bikes and some playing wrestling, and the girls playing jump rope and jumping jack. I see accidents and other things.

I hear kids calling and playing and fighting and singing and yelling and I see kids playing records and dancing and playing hide go seek and other games and smell food from someone's window and smell trash and smell apple pie and smell bad breath. And that's the truth.

I can smell garbage in the open lot and I can hear the train go by and hear airplanes go by and hear people talking together and hear birds and hear fire engines sometimes.

I would like to live in a house with ten rooms for all my kids and their kids and a husband and a maid and a poodle dog and five cats and a German shepherd dog. And two stories and two kitchens and three bathrooms and two living rooms with carpeting on all my rooms and a big dancing hall and a lovely jewelry box and sharp clothes and earrings and necklaces and bad shoes. And my kids wearing mean clothes and my husband. And each child with their own room and own bathroom.

I would like to live in a house by myself and I would like to have the teacher for my slave and I would like to give him a penny a week. That is all.

I would like to live in an apartment with an upstairs and a downstairs and a lot of pretty stuff and I would like different kinds of lights and hardwood floors and I would not like bad people in the building and would like pretty trees in front of the building.

I would like to live in a white house with white sink and white stove in it. I would like everything white, also my pots. Only thing I don't want white is my stereo.

I will like to live in the west. With wagon wheels for

the bannister. And have a horse and a ranch with some chickens and a cow and a pig. And live by myself. And it will be quiet.

––––––––

I like how the weather feels in fall. Also I like when the rain is falling in the night, it makes you feel warm and nice.

––––––––

It feels like it is snowing when the leaves fall and turn brown and yellow so when you touch them they crunch up to bits and you stand on them they do the same thing and you see squirrels run around the place and families are ready for winter.

––––––––

Too many leaves falling off the trees and the animals are going home and it's getting cooler and cooler but I had a lot of fun and I still play basketball and sports and other games. Pretty soon it will be snowing and ice cold and half of people will go to school and I will be glad when school is out, for I can have fun.

––––––––

In the fall all the leaves fall off the trees and the weather is like summer and winter at the same time. It is cold and sometimes it is hot or cool, but most of the time it is cold.

––––––––

If I was in jail I would yell my head off and then I would not say anything to anyone, not to my mother or my father or my sisters or brothers or cousins. Then when I got out I would kill everybody.

––––––––

If I went to jail it will be like going there for the rest of my life. And it will seem lonely and nobody to talk to. And it will seem boring and only looking at brick walls all day. And sleeping on a hard bed. And feeling stuffy and hot and feeling sad and like you're all alone and like the end of the world has come. And I will be thinking about what my parents think about me in jail and for nine months at that. And when I get out I will be so happy and so happy to smell fresh air and birds singing and seeing little kids playing and most of all seeing my family.

––––––––

If I went to jail for nine months I would look stupid sitting up there looking out the window and not getting enough sleep and all I would see is birds flying by and hear trucks and sometimes your friends come and visit you and the day I got out I wouldn't feel like leaving the jail house.

––––––––

If I ever go to jail I will not like to see anyone because if I go to jail for nine months when I get out the person that told on me would have to be killed. And then I would have to go some place where the police have no authority to take me away. And if they find me I will have to turn in my reputation and then I will break out. And when I get out I will have to start all over again and then I will live in the west and have a wife to cook and wash and bake and then I will be all right again.

––––––––

If I was in jail for nine months I would feel sometimes happy. I would think about how I could play outside if I wasn't held in jail with bars all around me. I would think about home and how I could be driving in my father's car, sometimes go and visit my family and friends, then come back home and rest on a cozy couch or bed. When I got out of prison I would feel free, going everywhere. I would be very happy to see my birds again, I like them very much. I would be able to feed them again and then let them fly away and in the evening they would come back.

––––––––

I think love is when you like a person but more than like. When you love a person you feel a lot for that person. Just like you love your mother and father and you have someone to go to. Love is like when you look at someone or something and all of a sudden you feel in love with that person or thing and you want that person to love you. Love is a thing that happens at first sight and you will begin to want that thing more than anything in the world.

––––––––

I think love is when you have someone to go to. And when you have a boyfriend. And someone to stick up for you. And when you die you will have a decent burial. And someone who would die for you and if you were accused of murder would say you were innocent. And when you are in the hospital they will come to visit you every day. And when your birthday comes you will get a present.

———

I would like to live in the west. I would get married and then I would have a farm and a ranch with my beautiful wife. Inside my house would be a psychedelic fireplace. And I will work at a milk farm where cows and horses and chickens and pigs are. And when I come home from work I will sit down in my chair and she will bring me my food. And after I get through I will go to bed.

———

When you care
about someone
and love them
and when he
is sad
you make
him happy
and you go
out on dates
and kiss
and have children
and then get
married.

———

Today is a rainy day and cold and wet. It makes things look wet and soggy. When you get under a tree rain falls right on you. And on rainy days the smell of leaves and the smell of grass smell good. The leaves shine out their colors and they look pretty in the rain, and houses and trees and sidewalks and cars and other things are wet. And the rain sounds like little snowflakes on a snowy day and it sounds like pretty little thumping on the top of the house and on the windows. And clouds are out today and it is cold and cloudy but a pretty day.

———

It makes me feel like
it's going
to be
a bad day
everything is
going wrong

I can smell
the bakery
and the bread
and
hear
the train

It was raining this morning and cars were screeching and dogs barking and I had to go to the school across the street and we had to tell the teacher something and then we smelled smoke because a car got blown up because it turned around and made flames.

This morning was a very bad morning to me. I had a headache and everything and when I came out to go to school it was raining and the cars were going fast.

The weather makes
me feel good
And the smell is dirty
But the sound is
spectacular

I woke up in the middle of the night and all of a sudden I smelled smoke but I paid no attention and my little sister Sheila said see the smoke. And I said What smoke, there is no smoke. And she said But there is some smoke, I see it. Just then the wind blew the smoke away and I said You're just tired and I took her to her room and read her a story and then she was sleepy too. I went to bed and my mother and father were out and I was minding the house. All of a sudden I heard a scream. I jumped out of bed and ran to my sister's room and there she was in the room blocked off by fire. So I got the rest of the kids up and they all were crying. What are we going to do about Sheila in the room? And we all got a pail of water and threw it on the fire and then it went out and I ran outside with all the kids and rang the firebox and the firemen came and said Is everybody out of the house? And we said Yes. And soon my mother and father came back and we were happy. And my mother said, I am proud of you.

One day in the summer I was watching TV. I watched

TV for a whole day and it was getting dark and I was still watching a movie about fire and I was scared but I watched the whole thing until it went off. It went off and I fell to sleep and slept, and slept, slept and slept, for six hours and suddenly I started burning up. I was hot and I couldn't sleep any more, and I felt a heat hit me so I jumped up to look because I smelled smoke and when I looked my brother was smoking and I had my clothes on. I got up and looked at the clock and it was 12 o'clock so I got under the cover and went to sleep.

———

I was playing outside and I asked my mother could I go to the movies tonight at 7:00 o'clock. Me and my sister went and left my mother at home. When we got out of the movie we saw a big big fire around my way and we ran home and saw our house was on fire. We said Take care, our mother is in there. But then we found out that she went to the shop with my father.

———

Halloween is the best thing in October. Halloween is a time to have fun, to get together in a group and go out. And it is a time to dress up in Halloween clothes and a mask, ugly or pretty. Some people are witches, ghosts, nurse, doctor, bum, Batman, Superman, vampires, and more. And Halloween is a time when you go to the door every minute to treat the kids and to hear them say trick or treat. And Halloween is when you stay out till 12 o'clock and go house to house. And you can even go to a Halloween party or have a Halloween party. And Halloween is scaring people and having fun until 12 o'clock. Halloween is a time to get together and have a ball.

———

Halloween is
when it
is very
dark
and the
people come
to your
home
and one
night

an old
lady gave
me an
apple
with
a razor
in it
But I
did not
know anything
about it
so I
did not eat
the apple
and I
gave it
to a dog
and the
dog bit it
and it
stuck in
his tongue
and then he went crazy and died.

———

One night
I was coming
Around the
corner
I was astonished
If I hadn't
scared
myself
so much maybe
my heart
would've
kept pumping
I was killed
The police
took me away
and I had a
funeral
Oct. 30, 1970
And my family was there too.

———

I wish I was a butterfly with lots of pretty colors, and

when someone tried to catch me I would fly away. I would stay in the air and fly all over the place, even to Atlanta, Georgia.

———

*I would like
being
a bluebird
it's fun being
a bluebird
would you
be a bluebird
with me*

———

I would like to be a chimpanzee, so I can play and have fun, climb trees and play with baby gorillas. I would be somebody's pet, so they could feed me and train me so when I get four years old and learn to write and eat, learn to count money and add and find me a friend when I get big they will take me back to Africa where I belong.

———

I would want to be a beautiful bird up in the air with lovely feathers on my wings. I will feel nice as if I've got the whole world for myself and people will be watching me and wishing I would be their friend. However I will not be alone.

———

If I were principal of the King School I would have the whole school doing stations and walking with no noise in the hall and no fighting or swearing. And every boy would have to wear a tie and no boy would be able to come to school without a tie and I wouldn't let them get away with anything. The girls too. And any time they get fresh with the teacher they will be punished and sent home.

———

And all the kids of the King will have respect to one another and no fighting or bad language or fresh talk to the principal or any teacher and that is the way it would be if I was the principal sitting in the office. And I would not have to worry because I would know that all the classes are working and learning a lot.

———

I would make all the classes in the school clean up their homeroom, and I would make one half for boys and one half for girls, and take all the bad children and put them in a special class, and I would change the chairs, and the coatroom, and the cafeteria.

———————

Snow is a thing that happens in the winter and covers the streets and sidewalks and houses and cars and trucks. And all the birds go to the south and the squirrels go out and get a pile of nuts and take them into trees and the bear sleeps for the whole winter and little kids and big kids are outside playing and having snowball fights and running and jumping in the snow and calling to their friends and the noise is so loud that it seems they will never shut up.

And the snow looks beautiful with everything sparkling and glowing and to see everything white and so pretty makes you feel happy. And when it begins to snow all the kids get on their coats and hats and shout out of the windows, It's snowing, It's snowing.

———————

If black slaves did not bring music to America, we would not know about soul music today. And if we did know about soul music, it would not be as good as it is. And if they had not brought dances to America, America would be standing still. And if they did not bring art to America, I don't think any artists would do as well. And if they did not bring slang language to America, it would be new to the black people too just as much as the white people when white kids use this language like she's hip. And if there was no slaves we would not even know of them. And the white people would have to work for themselves, and would have the poor white people for slaves.

———————

If I was a fly I would like to go to Paris, London, Moscow, Jamaica. I would like to roam all over the world, places that I have never been to in my life, and have a nice time with my friends that I meet. I would want to go everywhere. But I would not want to meet up with a spider and even if I was a fly I would still want to listen to music and see people dancing and laughing and talking and just having a nice time. And that is what I would want to do and want to hear and want to see if I was a fly.

If I was popular like the Jackson Five I would live in a big house with a dog and some mean furniture and carpeting on the floors. And I would get a charge to buy more and more records so I can become popular like the Jackson Five and everybody will like me and my group. And I will have lots of money.

I would not want to have an argument with the group because that will be very bad and that might break up the group and I will have to find a new group or sing by myself. And it will be very bad if I got sick and could not sing and if we get all messed up. And it will be bad if we went out of style, and lost all the money we had.

If I were popular the good things would be riding around in my limousine and meeting other famous people. The bad things are being killed by the bad guys and going in the hospital. That's all.

If I found an alien in my bedroom, I would be shocked. And once I got over it I would let him stay and let him do my dishes and do my homework and do my cleaning and do my hair and fix up my room and mop the floors and sweep the floor and go to the store for my mother and get my beatings! And when he is finished I would go outside and we would play and have fun and I would let him meet my friends. And I would teach him what he should do on this planet.

If I went into my bedroom and saw an alien sitting on my bed I would go and call the navy, the marines and the army and they would get that old alien and send him back where he came from and I wouldn't sleep in the bed any more.

I would not like to be an elephant because I would not like to eat so much and I would not want to get fat and be so smelly and I would not want to have to live with other fat elephants and have to look for food when you are hungry. And I would not want to have to sleep in the forest and not sleep in a bed. But I would be so mean that no one would ever come near me. And if a tiger or lion should attack me, I would stomp him to death. And I would not let any other kinds of animals beat me. But I would be scared of a mouse, because elephants are scared of mice.

If I was an elephant I'd roam all around the place. If I was an elephant I would be the king.

The police were looking for a man and the man was on drugs and he was running around loose. And one day they saw the man standing up on the corner. And when the man saw them he pulled out his gun and shot a policeman. And so a policeman went behind these houses to the other side of the street and shot the man out to the open street and they took the man to the hospital and they found out that the man who was shooting him out to the open, the policeman, that he did not shoot the man because there was no bullet mark on the man. And so they did an autopsy on the man and found out that the drug he took killed him. So the doctor said the accident was not caused by the policeman but by the drugs. And after the operation it was all in the papers the next day. And he had a family funeral in a big church and the boys that he hung around with, which was his gang, and his girlfriend came in a Cadillac.

There was this boy in the hospital for two years and his family saw him every two weeks. So anyway his mother keeps praying in church for her son to get out so the police can keep an eye on him. Because they think he got something to do with drugs. And his gang are teenagers and his girl thinks he is crazy. They are all standing looking at the body. The crazy died of an overdose. So everybody went to his funeral. The church had an organ and it played.

On the Christmas vacation I would just like to get up in the morning and have fun with my games and clothes and other things I get for Christmas. And my mother says to my little sisters she is going to leave out some presents for Santa. And they all get up in the morning and that is one day you do not see them fighting or kicking. And the night before Christmas there they are in the living room singing songs and soon they go to bed and dream about Christmas. And in the morning they are fighting to see which is which and grabbing and in the morning my mother is in the bed all tired. But I know why. And David knows why.

————

There was a snowball fight in our back yard and there were 20 girls and 21 boys. We were just throwing snowballs at each other. But one girl got hurt. A boy threw a snowball at her and it hit her and went down her throat. So she went to the hospital. The doctor told her that it was very serious and that she might die.

————

Dear Santa,
I hope you will have a very good Christmas. But don't forget to give me my Christmas tree. Good riddance, you fat over-grown hog.

————

Martin Luther King was a great man. He made many many speeches all over the world and he became famous. Martin had four kids and his wife's name was Coretta King. He lived in Alabama. He was making a speech in Alabama and he was shot in the neck and he died on April 4, 1968, and was buried on April 11, 1968. And I have a sister she was born on April 11, 1968 and she was named after Coretta King. My sister's name is Coretta.

————

Martin Luther King was a great old man. I don't think he was mean because he did all he can. He said, Let freedom ring, and let my people free. He might of been a bad man before. But not now.

————

Martin Luther King Jr. to me is a famous man who helped black people to get Civil Rights. He fought for Civil Rights, he fought worst than the men in Vietnam do. That is the reason why he got killed.

————

I think drugs are bad and people should not take them and some people can't help themselves from taking them. I hope no one never tricks me by putting something in my food because drugs can kill you and they make you do funny things like run out in front of a car and the car might kill you. So is my family concerned about drugs, my mother told me and the rest don't take drugs.

When you die you go in a dream for one hundred years and then you get a look at the world hundred years later and you see how the world has changed and the kind of car that goes to the moon and you get to see your great grandson but you can not talk to him and if you touch him he will not feel it and in the end you go back in the ground and go back in a sleep for a very long time.

Death will be like taking an overdose of LSD you feel fine like sleeping forever.

My Mom's mother died when it was her birthday. She got sick and all of us went to buy her something and she took it with a pain when we came back she were on the ground dead. We all got frightened that time I was five years old and I saw her lying on the floor and I beat her and the police came and I said I did just beat her because she was on that floor sleeping for an hour when they put her in that box she die laughing anyhow everybody's turn will come to die.

Four men went to the back of the house and they started talking and arguing at each other. Then two of them got in a car and drove, and the other two got in another car and drove after them tearing them sharp corners and shouting so loud people looked out of the window and heard the shouting and someone call the cops and came after them. The cops was going so fast that you could not see them. The fight went on and on then the fight came to an end and the cops caught them and took them down station.

As I walk down the street a man shot me. I fell to the ground and it went black. Then I heard a lot of talk- ing and crying. I heard siren motor and then I felt me riding in a car. Then I seen a red face and a white face and I said you the devel and you god. I want to go with you god and the devel said your bleeding let me fix you up. Then every thing went black and I die and something cut me and open my eyes and the doctor ran away. The end. No remarks.

———

This is a real story. My cousin died two weeks ago but she was weak anyways. She died in her sleep and when they had the funeral her hair was straight and curly. But I don't know why people are sad when other people die they are sad I think they should be glad to get people out of this dirty world.

———

In fifty years it will be a place of creatures. It is going to be more killing than there is now, more people on drugs and inventing more harmful things and dirty smelly pollution, trash, glass and bottles everywhere and trash all in the streets and more bad accidents and more invention that will try and improve the bad things but then it is going to be too late. And nobody is going to want to help clean up because they are going to be so dirty theirselves. And houses all run down. And parks messy and the air is going to have all kinds of smells in it. And pollution everywhere you watch. And more crimes and other bad things and kids outside all time of night all high and having drugs.

———

There is more than just a black color. There are many more colors. Black is a nigger with a little Afro or sometimes a big Afro. I would like to be a black astronaut or a painter or a black rep at the Boston Garden at the wrestling star or a black school principal. Or might be part of a black band playing as a drummer or a student council, but we still in peace, black don't mean nothing to me.

———

The most beautiful thing in the world is girls, because their mothers, big sisters, or guardians could comb their hair make them look nice and dressed up really good and just try to make girls the most beautiful thing in the world. Some mothers and guardians don't care how their kids look as long as they look pretty they send them out in rags, bags, and even snags. They are full of stunk junk and of bunk. But I will care.

———

The first day I ever went to school in Trinidad I had a white teacher she hated all black she use to give us a lot of beating and it was the last day of school and we had a party she took me and our friends to the class and she beated us all. I did not even know what she beat us for.

———

I had teachers that made me feel cheap and I didn't learn anything from them. They would talk about us right there in front of our face and talk to another teacher and talk about us like we were nothing at all. Just like we were not there. And every time I would do my work better than a white kid that white kid always got the Oh how good, this is very very nice, your mother should be proud of you. But then I got mine right and neatly handwriting the teacher say she just says good with a funny look.

———

If I heard on the radio that the world was about to end I would go right to my bed and sit on it when the day come I would say come and get me because I'm ready to die.

———

I don't know what other people would do but I would get my family and my friends together and start swimming my way to Africa.

———

My hair is nappy
My soul is happy
I'm black and I'm proud

———

Seven.

Getting It All Together
in Grade 6-D

I began my third year at the King School with much less trepidation than the second. I felt that the learning stations were bound to work if I was flexible enough and kept the standard of the material up, and I concentrated on improving the physical layout of the room. My class was 6-D, an expression of confidence from the administration since I had been entrusted with one of the "academic" sections. By November I had accumulated a class of twenty-six kids, and I was struck by how little difference there was between this class and 6-G the year before. Despite the tracking system, both were filled with bright, attractive kids; both had their share of problems.

Within the first month I got rid of all the desks in the room and replaced them with large plywood tables. This proved to be a very cheap way (at seven-and-a-half dollars a table) of creating large amounts of very flexible workspace and making the room seem bigger and quieter (the latter because we could do without all the clanking and banging of the old desks). The tables are eight feet long and four feet wide and five-eighths of an inch thick, and rest on three-foot-high cardboard cylinders which the International Paper factory in Framingham discards every day.

At first the kids had fun sanding down the edges and decorating the surfaces with a myriad of designs, names, and other thoughts. After a while the surfaces of the tables got cluttered with these inscriptions and began to get dirty, so the kids suggested painting them. Within a few weeks almost all the tables were

painted as huge flags — most of them the black, red, and green of the black nationalist flag.

There were six tables, one of them for the three typewriters and a resource area with all the games and puzzles, and the other five for groups of kids. The tables lent much more cohesiveness to the groupings the kids had made for themselves, since no one could split apart or be rejected from a group and become isolated by moving an individual desk away from the group. The tables also gave people more room to work, and allowed them to spread out and separate from each other while still sitting in a cozy clique.

Another major change was ripping out the closet doors in the back of the room and installing a four-level, twelve-foot-long bookcase. I went and bought some exciting paperbacks and raided my mother's house for other interesting books from Peanuts to picture books on nature and the First World War. I then put all the books on the shelves with their covers facing outward, so that the color and appeal of the paperback jackets was working with me to get the kids reading. (As it turned out, this was not enough, and in November I started a compulsory one-book-a-week program with a book report every Friday.)

After building the bookcase, I put the rug down in the corner next to it and put a magazine rack and filing cabinet on the other side of the rug as a kind of room divider. The typewriter, game table, and rug created a whole section of the room that was devoted to "fun" activities, while the rest of the room was filled with worktables. The division was appropriate and worked well, although the "play" area was perhaps still too noisy for enough reading to take place. At one point I considered buying acoustical tile for the ceiling to deaden the sound in the room somewhat, but decided it was too expensive and would spoil the kids, allowing them to talk louder than they would be able to in other classrooms.

I then bought games and puzzles — Monopoly, Stratego, Scrabble, Quizmo, Soma, Battleship, and many others — and built a lot of small cubbyholes in the middle of the typewriter table to accommodate all

of them and other jigsaw puzzles, flash cards, and word games.

With the tables, the bookcase, books, games, and a few more posters, my expenses came to about two hundred dollars (I had spent around a hundred dollars my first year). A little under half of this was covered by a grant from the Educational Collaborative of Greater Boston; the rest came from my own pocket, and from my income from the two magazine articles I had written about my first two years. Some teachers feel that this is about what you should spend out of your own income each year (Steven Daniels suggests a policy of "Teaching on $2.00 a day" in his book, *How 2 Gerbils, 20 Goldfish, 200 Games, 2,000 Books and I Taught Them How to Read*). But clearly there are a lot of teachers with more commitments and less outside income than I had for whom this is grossly unfair. The Philadelphia public schools recently started giving every teacher in the system twenty-five dollars in cash at the beginning of each year to spend on their classrooms. This is not enough, but is a step in the right direction. Perhaps every principal should have discretion over a certain amount of money which could be dispensed to any teacher who submitted a reasonable proposal.

With Grade 6-D I started the learning stations on the second day of school, went through the stage of moving around from station to station, and settled the class into smoothly-functioning groups at five tables. Writing the station worksheets proved a much less arduous task the second year, although there were so many chances to introduce fresh material and improve old material that I found myself in no danger of becoming bored with writing them. I kept one copy of the first year's stations, and was able to improve on them and add to them when I felt creative and fall back on them when I didn't. In my third year my material was meatier and longer and I covered more topics more quickly, but I still tried to "tune" the work to the class day by day.

One change I made was that the Creative Writing was no longer on a sheet like the other station worksheets. Instead, I wrote the title suggestion for the day on one of the remaining patches of usable blackboard at the beginning of the day, and the kids wrote a page every other day in spiral notebooks. This way they could see their progress, and I could get into more of a written give-and-take with them when I read the books. They were not required to write on the topic, and they could copy out of a book if they didn't feel like writing something original. The theory of this comes from Daniel Fader *(Hooked on Books)* — that any writing is better than none and kids will eventually build up enough confidence to launch out on their own writing after they have copied for a while.

One innovation in the learning station sheets was that I numbered each one and had the kids file them in loose-leaf binders when the previous day's work was corrected. This not only gave them good experience in organizing themselves and a feeling of the cumulative work of the year, but also proved the only way to keep the tables neat since with no desks there was no other place to put papers.

With the stations somewhat meatier and with all the other things there were to do in the classroom, the station time easily filled most of the day, overcoming in a stroke the amorphous residual time that sometimes bothered me the year before. Aside from the correcting at the end of the day, I addressed the whole class not more than five or ten minutes, usually in thirty-second bursts when something came up that I wanted to share with everyone. I continued to use the tape recorder and lyrics of songs in odd moments at the beginning and end of days.

The kids were in the room much more than was 6-G because of cutbacks in Art and Industrial Arts and Gym periods and because the Spanish teacher preferred to come to our room and work individually with the kids rather than fighting the whole group in her room. At any given moment in the day, most of the facilities of the room were being used. Walking into the room you would find perhaps half the class busy at work on the station worksheets, some alone, some with groups of friends, some at the tables, others sprawled on the rug; a few kids playing Monopoly and Stratego, one or two doing jigsaw puzzles, a few reading books, three pounding away on the typewriters, and a few talking with me or fooling around. I spent my time the same way I had the first year of stations — talking to individuals or small groups, helping people with their work, and prodding people who didn't look as though they were going to get through it before the end of the day. The atmosphere through most of the day was serene and friendly, with occasional altercations (usually about my "bugging" them about their work) and occasional noisy days when nobody seemed to be in a very good mood.

So basically the year saw the fleshing out of the potential of the learning stations. This process can go on for several more years; there is always something else that can be done in such a flexible setting. Some items on the agenda are: gerbils and fish in the room; curtains in the windows; flower boxes in the windows; more comfortable furniture in the reading area; and many more math and science games and projects. One exciting development was that in November two parents (the mother and aunt of a girl in the class) volunteered to help in the room on a full-time basis. They were initially attracted by the station worksheets the girl was bringing home (especially those dealing with current events such as the Attica State Prison rebellion). They visited the class after school, and then came in several times during school. They were so impressed by the atmosphere that they wanted to help; the idea was entirely their own, and I naturally embraced it. Their presence in the room was an enormous boom — it allowed us to pay much greater attention to kids with problems in certain areas, and brought new people with different experiences and viewpoints into the room.

Alas, this did not last. Both women became enmeshed in domestic problems (lead poisoning of young children at home, pressure from the Welfare Office to get a job), and had to leave after only a month. But they had made a sizable contribution and showed me the possibilities of using parents in the classroom.

Perhaps even more important than this development was the creeping impact of the learning stations on the rest of the school. At least five teachers in the building were strongly influenced by the system by seeing it in operation, talking to me, and reading my worksheets, and variations of the system appeared in their classrooms. Each teacher developed his or her own style of running the station idea; all slowly moved towards a more open and flexible setup. Even some classrooms without learning stations got typewriters, bookcases, and tables and allowed kids more freedom to use their time in such unstructured activities. Other teachers came into my room and were impressed by the atmosphere of freedom and intense involvement. There was virtually no criticism of the system, and the level of acceptance seemed to rise every day.

I also started circulating my station worksheets to all the sixth-grade teachers every day, and many of the other teachers quietly used the material or their own variations of it. Since I felt inadequate as an Art teacher and had very little idea how to use audio-visual aids, I got ideas from my colleagues in those areas in return for my worksheets.

I continued to take kids on field trips, and although it seemed that they had been more places than the kids in 6-G (a reflection of favoritism in the tracking system?), these were still very successful.

The school as a whole continued to be threatened by various forces. In October, intruders who came in to look for a boy who had been antagonizing their eighth-grade sister ran afoul of three young teachers and seriously beat them. There was a rash of false fire alarms in the fall, and countless pleas to deactivate some of the alarm boxes and bring in a security patrol were ineffective. During false fire alarms, and when the kids were outside for several real fires, there were numerous fights and on one occasion an ugly confrontation with firemen and policemen. Several teachers quit, unable to cope with the atmosphere of violence and disruption, the oppressively heavy teaching load, and the lack of equipment and materials and solutions. Others were worn down physically and psychologically to the point where they were unable to make the emotional investment necessary to innovate. Yet veteran teachers who had been in the school when it was still the Campbell School told us that our present troubles were only one eighth as bad as they had been before the black administration came in.

This was small consolation to us as a number of truly crazy kids wandered around the school threatening to shoot and knife teachers and other students, getting none of the attention and treatment they so badly needed. The situation continued to deteriorate. One Sunday, the entire school was vandalized; almost every room was turned upside down by intruders whose only objective seemed to be destruction. Other intruders constantly stole equipment. The lack of security in the school made it more difficult for teachers to invest time and money in their classrooms. During the day it was a constant struggle to keep a number of older kids in their classes; they preferred to roam through the halls disrupting other classes and looking for action. Often they found it in physical confrontations with teachers, and the school had some of its worst days when groups of teachers spent the entire day in court.

Of course there were many good things going on in the school as well. There were days when the relationship between students and the staff seemed downright friendly, when it was easy to say that the problems of the school were caused by a small group of demented troublemakers. The principal established firm, confident, and efficient leadership against overwhelming odds, and showed tolerance for a grassroots movement for classroom innovation — which appeared to be as far as the constraints of her position would allow her to go. And many parents seemed willing to support the school, some to the point of coming in as volunteers. Yet the future of the school is very much in doubt.

Perhaps the *worst* thing that can happen to the King School would be for the present holding action to drag on — for us to continue merely surviving each week without a catastrophe. Most people believe that only a major crisis — a bomb explosion or a murder — will bring the kind of attention, funding, and willingness to innovate that the school so desperately needs; while hardly wishing for such a crisis, they doubt that there are nonviolent ways of changing the school, and lapse into cynicism about the future.

It is easy to blame this situation on racism, inequality, the Boston School Committee, and other scapegoats, but how do you begin to change it? A good deal of federal money has gone through the school over the last three years with little impact, and under present conditions even a massive input of money might be wasted. Instead, what is needed is a very strategic allocation of money and manpower to get new ideas and approaches growing in the school to the point where they can sustain themselves and gain the support of the community.

As a small step in this direction, I plan to use a certain amount of the income from this book to help teachers to innovate and to stimulate various positive activities in the school.

But my most important activity remains teaching kids and demonstrating to their parents and to other teachers that there are specific methods that can make a classroom rigorous, stimulating, and fun.

Eight.

Learning Stations:

An Analysis

Despite many ups and downs, and despite my own tendency to drop projects halfway and not follow through with things, the learning station system that evolved during the first month of my second year has worked well ever since. In retrospect it seems clear that it was not I who kept the system going (although I worked hard at it) but rather the kids, and that they did so because it appealed to them in some very important ways.

The system has four major differences from conventional classrooms:
1. Kids sit in groups spread around the room rather than in rows.
2. Worksheets in seven subject areas (Math, English, Social Studies, Spelling, Creative Writing, General, and Reading) are put in pockets scattered around the outside of the room every morning Monday through Thursday.
3. On these station days, the students are free to move around the room and do the worksheets in any order they like as long as they finish all seven by the end of the day.
4. The teacher's role is not one of controlling the class or teaching seven subjects (or even one) at the front of the room, but rather: (a) writing worksheets for seven subjects the night before and running off copies first thing in the morning; (b) moving around the room during the station time helping people with the work and any other problems; (c) planning other activities for the remaining part of the day after the

stations are finished; (d) correcting the stations with the whole class in the last hour of the day; and (e) evaluating progress in the traditional subjects with tests every Friday.

Why did the learning stations appeal to us so strongly? In terms of learning, how does a morning of stations compare with a conventional class, so many of which alienate kids and result in constant struggles for their attention and cooperation? Certainly just about anything would compare favorably with my disastrous attempt at conventional teaching in my first year, but how does this arrangement compare with a *good* conventional class in which the teacher is reasonably imaginative and in control? Was it merely the novelty of the stations that made them a success, or were other factors — my experience and improved knowledge of the kids and the school — responsible for an atmosphere in Grade 6-G that had little to do with the learning stations? In short, is there anything in them that can be recommended to other teachers?

It seems to me that there are nine basic types of activity that go on in almost all classrooms. The fifth on the list below is the midpoint; above it the activities are increasingly important to learning, and below it they are increasingly a waste of the kids' time. Perhaps someday someone will be able to do a time-and-motion study comparing a learning station class with a conventional class on these criteria:

1. Pupil-minutes working things out for themselves
2. Pupil-minutes working individually with the teacher
3. Pupil-minutes working with other students on schoolwork
4. Pupil-minutes actively taking part in a group discussion
5. Pupil-minutes talking with other students on non-academic subjects
6. Pupil-minutes doing meaningless, repetitive paperwork
7. Pupil-minutes passively listening to a discussion or a teacher
8. Pupil-minutes watching or participating in "discipline" conflicts with the teacher

9. Pupil-minutes doing nothing, whether sitting in silence or fooling around

Other things being equal, I am convinced that the station class would be way ahead on the first three items and the fifth, while the conventional class would be ahead on the last three. This is because the station class is geared to letting kids work things out for themselves, because it frees the teacher from discipline conflicts that gobble up the time of the whole class, and because stations can help kids individually when they are not helping themselves in their groups. The station class also provides greater flexibility for discussions throughout the day, thus increasing the amount of active class participation as opposed to passive listening to a teacher's "command performance" at the front of the room.

Grade 6-G was probably quite high on item 9 (fooling around doing nothing) because I didn't provide enough stations and enough things to do when people finished them. This improved in my third year with the games, puzzles and books. As for item 6, the amount of busywork depends on the teacher in both kinds of classes. It is easy to see how a learning station class could slide into using a lot of meaningless paperwork as an easy way out of more stimulating worksheets; some of my stations verged on this category, and I would have benefited from working with a team of other sixth-grade teachers to pool our ideas and interests and keep the standard of the worksheets higher. But conventional classes are equally open to the temptations of busywork, especially to calm down an energetic class and avoid the complications of getting kids overexcited about subjects.

Item 3 (kids helping each other with their work) is a particularly important element of the station class and one which is seldom present in more tightly-controlled conventional classes. Some educators feel that kids learn much more rapidly from their peers than from teachers, and when classwork is more or less self-instructing, as the station worksheets were, this process is facilitated. There is the added advantage that students who have a grudge against a teacher at any particular moment can still get help from their friends or figure the work out by themselves.

As for item 5 — kids talking to each other about movies, fights, girls, the Jackson Five, and so on — there is less agreement among educators about the academic benefits. Some say that there is plenty of time for this outside of school. But I feel that, with the traditional subjects and much more being covered during the day, we could afford to have more unrelated conversations going in the room; there is little to be lost, and it is likely that a whole process of social orientation and personality development may be going on all the time at a completely different level than it does outside the school. In other words, the informality of the station time both seems to make the work less of a burden and creates a positive informality around more academic subjects, which allows learning to flourish in a more tranquil, congenial environment.

So even with the many weaknesses of my learning station methods, the system seems to be ahead of conventional teaching on the most important indices of the scale above. While a brilliant conventional teacher might be able to do as well or better in terms of involvement by the kids and moving around the room to help individuals, most teachers who try to dominate the activities of a classroom will inevitably bore the kids a lot of the time and become involved in time-consuming "discipline" or discipline-avoidance activities. Moreover, it seems to me that even if a good conventional teacher explains something to a class orally from the front of the room and everyone seems to understand, it is not going to sink in as deeply as if the kids worked it out for themselves on individual worksheets.

Teaching a station class is certainly not easier than conventional teaching. It provides no magic shortcuts to the problems of the kids or the job of teaching them skills and concepts. It merely provides a better setting in which to do these things. The system requires hard work during school, almost two hours writing stations after school, and a willingness to forego iron control of activities in the classroom and to put up with a certain level of noise. It also demands an ability to pull the class together at certain points for correcting, discussions, and tests. But the station class has clear structural advantages over conventional classes, which add up to far more pupil-minutes in the first three indices mentioned above, and a much livelier, faster-moving, freer, and more cheerful environment.

Besides these fundamental advantages, the station class offers a number of other features.

One that needs further discussion is the atmosphere the stations create in the class. Because I was not straining to control the class and did not insist on silence, the room was relaxed and natural. The kids talked to each other as they did outside the school (with the swearing somewhat curtailed), and I was casual and colloquial in the way I talked to them. This meant that every day the community, with its problems and strengths, entered more fully into the classroom with the kids. The kids related to one another on their own terms, in their own way; they were themselves, and I accepted them for what they were. Because I did, they accepted me, and we liked each other. I don't mention this atmosphere to paint a picture of an idyllic relationship between me and the kids — clearly it wasn't — but because I think such an atmosphere makes good educational sense.

Many people would say that if you let kids be themselves in school, they will never learn anything, because schoolwork is no fun and school is a bore. This is a self-fulfilling prophecy if there ever was one, and by rejecting it I found the opposite to be true. In the relaxed atmosphere of the station time, I was able to meet the kids halfway with what they had to learn in school and a great deal more, and I found them really eager to learn almost all of it. Presented obliquely through the learning stations, rather than being forced on them in lockstep lecture classes, the work was fun to do even when it was humdrum Math and English, because these "dry" subjects were balanced by other less formal subjects and activities. The kids' attitude toward me on any given day didn't stop them from getting the work done. (One day a girl who had

a gripe with me wrote "I hate you" at the top of each of her seven immaculately finished stations. Imagine the disruption she would have caused had I been running a conventional class!). In the station-time atmosphere, the kids were more confident in coming to grips with the work (which was itself chattier and less threatening on the worksheets I had written) because they were surrounded by friends who would help them, because they could get my help almost any time, and because they were situated in a climate which was so relaxed and true to life that it helped them to be less tense and have a higher opinion of themselves and their abilities. Perhaps this is why they were able to involve themselves so much in the work and do so much of it, and why despite the amount they were doing they seldom felt burdened by it. Thus the station system was itself a way of coming to grips with the difficult problems of low self-esteem engendered by the system of tracking and other factors in the school and the community.

Besides its academic merits, this atmosphere in the room bred sound friendships. Throughout the year I enjoyed watching these blossom — sometimes the kids just sat and talked, other times they turned out pages of work in tandem.

Second, conventional classes put themselves at a serious disadvantage by trying to teach something to an entire class at the same time, in lockstep. Every kid's attention span and learning rate is different, and every student's style of learning is unique. Each will reach the "Oh, I see!" point at a different moment when something is being described, and even the most brilliant stand-up teacher can't synchronize these individual moments for a class of twenty-five. A station class doesn't even try to synchronize them. With the worksheets leading most of the kids most of the way through an explanation, and with the class doing them in each person's own order and at his own speed, the critical learning moments are scattered through the morning. When someone needs help, it is when the question is ripe in his mind, and he can usually get a hint or a prod from the teacher just at this critical point to nudge him to his own "Oh, I see!" point. Thus, while the material isn't that much more individualized than it might be in a conventional class, the way the kids approach it is highly individual, and the teacher's time is much more efficiently used because he makes his input at the point at which it is most productive and makes enough of an input to bring each kid to a full understanding.

This struck me with particular force one afternoon when I was helping George and Calvin with some Math after school. Both of them started to get excited about it at the same time, and I found it impossible to deal with both of them at once. Each wanted my full attention and needed every ounce of encouragement I could give. I had to shift quickly back and forth between them for five minutes, juggling them, and both of them got quite angry with me because this way I wasn't able to satisfy either of them. If it is this hard for just two boys after school, how much harder for an entire class! If a group of twenty-five kids gets excited about a subject at the same time (a rare occurrence, which is the product of fine teaching), you are just going to have to suppress a lot of that excitement and prevent most of the kids in the class from actively participating. On the other hand, if the kids don't get excited or involved in the subject, which is more common, they won't learn as much. In a station class the excitement is spread through the morning, and with luck and a lot of energy you can give kids your full attention, just for them, when they really need it, and try to stimulate interest and involvement where it has not been generated by the material. I almost always talked to kids alone, and when I spoke with a group or the whole class, it was briefly and at a time when they were really interested and willing to listen to me.

Another obvious advantage of the station system is the ability it breeds in the kids to work on their own, the ability to face a sheet of paper with specific directions on it and not be fazed, but follow them properly (which among other things will be an asset when they encounter standardized achievement tests, College Boards, and so forth). At the beginning of the year I found many of the kids, even the brightest, almost unable to do this. They were typical products of the teacher-dominated classroom, and for a while I had to hold their hands and explain even the simplest directions to them while I tried to wean them from their dependence on the teacher to do their thinking for them. At first I kept the stations very simple and charged around the room helping people at every stage, but within a month or so the kids got very good at working on their own, and I was able to explain fairly complex things to most of them on paper. By the end of the year almost everyone in the class was nonchalant about doing seven pages of closely-typed work, without my help, in two and a half hours, and some took a fierce pride in their total independence from me. Furthermore, this quality of independence extended outside the station time, as I discovered the morning I came in unprepared and the class organized itself around reading plays and working independently on other projects.

While the opportunities for copying other people's work were much greater in such a free classroom, the system struck at the basic reasons why kids "cheat": it made them feel more comfortable and sure of themselves; it provided an atmosphere that was less competitive and pressured; it challenged them to figure things out for themselves; and it provided work that was not boring or stale but geared to their specific aptitude, experiences, and interests.

The stations also bred a sense of responsibility. The kids were free to talk and wander around the room, but that was within the limits of a long-range obligation to finish all the stations. During the usual station time there was a tremendous amount of talking, hair-combing, fooling, and daydreaming, but almost every kid still found his or her own way of getting all the work done as well.

All but three people in the class reacted very well to this particular combination of freedom and responsibility. I treated them as adults, and they reacted as adults. This is partly why I had trouble conducting conventional classes later in the day, if the subject matter was less than scintillating, and why other teachers who taught my class sometimes found the kids difficult: certain kinds of conventional teaching seemed Mickey Mouse to the kids after the station time. However, my class was by no means the only one on the sixth-grade wing that felt this way, and I did not feel that it was only the stations that had hardened my class against conventional teaching.

A further advantage of the stations was that they were in and of themselves a reading program. Assuming that the best way to improve reading skills is to read a lot, the stations were great practice; they provided a great deal of material every day, together with a need to read it to find out what to do. I found that my students came into the school with excellent oral comprehension from television and an oral culture; when I explained or described something interesting out loud their retention was excellent. So to explain ideas orally would only have been using a skill they already had, while written explanations on the stations forced them to get ideas and concepts through the printed word — and thus were an effective tool in developing reading skills. Besides this, many of them read parts of stations out loud to each other and to me during the day. No doubt their increased ability to do work on their own was partly a result of improvements in their reading, and vice versa. (They were also taught Reading more conventionally — phonics, syllabification, and so forth — in a special Reading class and occasionally in my Spelling and English stations.)

Similarly, the stations gave the kids a great deal of practice in writing. There was more written work in our class than most other classes covered in much more time. When I asked them at the end of the year whether they thought their writing had improved, most of them thought it had. The daily Creative Writing station was especially important in making writing less of a threat and the expression of ideas on paper less painful and more natural.

Unfortunately I did not gather any before-and-after testing data to back up either of these claims about reading and writing. I realize I should do this in the future.

Another advantage of the stations was the range of different kinds of work they provided, from simple Spelling exercises that almost everyone could do without a mistake to the open-ended Creative Writing topics. Each kid could blend the different kinds of work according to his mood and his need for stability or adventure at that moment, so the curriculum was in a sense self-adjusting. In retrospect I don't think I provided *enough* of a range of activities, and I think the system will benefit greatly from the introduction of more activities.

There is another advantage to the variety of work going on at the same time in a station class. When I was in school I often balked when I was doing the same thing all the other kids in the class were doing, when I was being led in lockstep through some worksheet or lecture by the teacher, and this tendency increased as I became more individualistic. It struck me as being a childish and somewhat insulting process, and I often resisted whatever was being taught, even if it interested me, by fooling around, talking, or looking out the window to "keep my cool." But when a teacher gave me something to do on my own that was different from what everyone else was doing, I almost invariably became more excited and involved and worked harder. This dynamic (while it may not be equally important for everyone) is constantly at work in the station class. With seven different pieces of work being done in the course of the morning in different sequences, there are few people doing the same thing at any given moment, so kids feel more on their own, more like they are working it out for themselves, and it is that much easier to get involved.

Furthermore, the stations lifted some of the pedagogical burden from my shoulders and allowed me to relate to the kids at a more human level. As I mentioned earlier, few teachers, and even fewer kids, are really interested in a great deal of Math and English grammar and some of the more traditional topics in Social Studies. While they realize that there is no way to avoid learning such material, they find it hard to take it very seriously — that is something that is left to specialists in universities and to textbook writers. Teachers who fight for control in lecture classes in these subjects put themselves in the position of being not only boring but somewhat absurd, and confuse the kids about their identity as humans. I "cheated" by teaching the humdrum subjects mostly through self-instructing worksheets, which I wrote the night before (and tried to make as relevant and entertaining as possible), and which were more fun to do in the general atmosphere of the class even though they weren't inherently that interesting. I seldom talked to the class as a whole on subjects that did not interest both the kids and me. Thus the skills were taught, but we were able to relate to each other on a more comfortable, human level.

The stations had an added benefit for kids who finished more quickly than others. In a conventional class, those who are quicker at doing work than others generally have to stare into space for five or ten minutes while they wait for everyone else to finish. Even if a teacher provides games, books, or activities for them, there is not enough time to get involved, since the next lesson has to begin soon. In a station morning, on the other hand, these faster students accumulate the time they gain throughout the morning; if they gain five minutes on other kids on each station, they have gained thirty-five minutes by the end of the morning. This is a big enough chunk of time to get really involved in something else when they are finished.

A further advantage of the stations is that they are not expensive to run. Virtually the only expenses are duplicating masters, pencils, and copying paper (about 850 sheets a week last year), all of which most schools supply up to a point. (I reached that point in February last year and had to buy these three things myself.) If I had been refunded for the textbooks and other materials I did *not* use during the year, I would have probably "saved" enough money to cover this increment and some of the "frills" (field trips, posters, typewriters, and so forth) that I added to the stations. Without having made any precise calculations, I would guess that the per-pupil cost was about the same as in other Boston classrooms, but I feel that the dollars and cents were allocated more effectively.

During the station time it was also much easier to have visitors in the room. Although I was often worried about what they would think about the way I was running the class, I was able to dispel doubts and an-

swer criticisms by taking visitors under my wing for a ten-minute guided tour of the room. It was pleasant to be able to do this without disrupting the activities of the class, and visitors had a chance to see the class actually at work. They were always impressed by what they saw.

The same was true of the two parents who helped in the room for a month in my third year. With such a flexible and open environment, they fitted right in and were able to develop their own style of handling kids and their own set of relationships without my feeling undermined or threatened. Indeed, the more helpers and parents and student teachers there are in this kind of classroom, the better the quality of teaching will be, since there will be more viewpoints and more experiences for the kids to draw upon. In the future I plan to work toward what I consider the ideal arrangement: one or more parents and a student teacher in the room with me all the time.

Besides the help parents and student teachers can give a teacher, working in this kind of classroom can also be an eye-opening experience for the helpers. The two parents who worked in my room had never seen anything other than a traditional classroom, but very quickly became enthusiastic advocates of the learning stations and loved being in the room watching the kids, laughing with them, arguing with them, and helping them with their work. One of the parents urged the teacher of her other child to start running her class like mine, while the other parent began to think seriously about going back to school and becoming a teacher herself. Both had good ideas, criticisms, and suggestions for me about the class.

As for student teachers, an apprentice role in a learning-station classroom seems to me to be the only way that they can decide how they will teach and how to avoid the kind of first-year experience I had.

Finally, the stations suggested a way to answer some of the arguments for tracking kids into different classes by ability. Grade 6-G was a mixture of ability levels minus the brightest kids, who had been streamed into the top four "academic" sections. The rationale often given for this separation of different ability levels is that it is hard for a teacher to run a conventional class when kids in it are at different levels. The common complaint is that the class has to move at the pace of the slowest kids, to avoid leaving them behind. The station class, on the other hand, is flexible enough to handle a wide variety of ability levels, and in fact benefits from such a variety by giving the brighter kids a chance to help those who are having trouble as well as giving the teacher more freedom to do so. More station classes would allow schools to break up the damaging, invidious system of tracking and make variety into a virtue. The brighter kids would hardly be held back by this situation if the material in the class were flexible enough. The kids might even benefit more than they would from a more homogeneous class by having the opportunity to teach and learn from their peers.

There are three different approaches to meeting diverse academic needs in a learning-station classroom, each with its own appeal. The first (which is what I have done so far) is to have one set of worksheets every day, geared to the upper middle portion of the class, and give enough individual help during the day to bring slower kids up to that level. The second approach is to have a common set of materials but allow kids to proceed at their own pace, doing only the stations they feel competent to do well. (This means having a stock of worksheets in a filing cabinet and a prepared set of unit tests that kids can take when they have mastered a unit.) The third approach is to have a stock of worksheets at several different ability levels, so that kids can work on materials geared specifically to their Reading and Math levels.

There are disadvantages to all three approaches. The first depends very heavily on the teacher getting around the class, being sensitive to individual problems, and delivering the different amounts of help required to get kids of diverse abilities through a common set of materials. The second approach means that kids are working on different parts of the curriculum and would be less likely to help each other with their work than they would with the first approach.

It would also mean that some people would fall behind and never cover some topics, and feel left out of the mainstream of the class. The disadvantage of the third approach is that a multilevel set of materials is not available on the market and would take a long time to develop. If it were written in advance, as would probably be necessary because of the amount of work involved, it would not have the advantages of freshness and immediacy contained by worksheets written the night before.

With certain reservations, I feel that the first approach is the best way to meet academic needs in a heterogeneous classroom. The teacher has to be acutely aware of which kids need more help than others and be able to deliver the different amounts of help needed by different kids. But if a teacher feels able to do this, having the class do the same worksheets each day has a number of advantages.

First, it gives everyone in the class a feeling that he is in the mainstream, that the day's work is a group enterprise as well as an individual one. This is especially important for kids who have developed an inferiority complex by being put in "dumb" classes and given "special" work because they couldn't keep up with the rest.

Second, this approach makes it possible to correct the day's work as a class (which would not be possible if kids were at different points in the curriculum). This adds to the feeling of a group enterprise, gives an opportunity for group discussions on a body of shared experience, gives kids quick feedback on their work, and minimizes the amount of correcting the teacher has to do after school (which is very important for teachers who are exerting themselves emotionally and physically during the day).

Third, this approach means that the teacher (or a team of teachers) can concentrate the night before on writing one set of materials that are fresh and attuned to the interests and abilities of the class at that moment. Not having a lot of correcting to do means that there is more time to work on these materials and make them really good, and writing them the night before means they will probably be better than materials written months before.

Fourth, having the whole class do the same worksheets means that brighter kids are much more likely to help friends who are having trouble with the work than if they were working on different parts of the curriculum or different-level worksheets. This means that good peer-group learning is likely to fill in where the teacher doesn't have the time to reach and supplement the teaching he does. This may be better for both brighter and slower kids than working alone at their own level.

Finally, this approach presents a real challenge to slower kids to catch up, to join the mainstream of the class. If it is presented in the right way, and if the teacher and brighter kids can give the necessary help and encouragement, this challenge is one that most underachieving kids will respond to very well. My experience over the past two years has borne this out with only a few exceptions.

The approach becomes even stronger if kids have the chance to go back and re-do units that they failed. This was always possible on my flexible grade charts. The approach is also strengthened if the station worksheets are themselves flexible, containing a core which everyone in the class does and then tangents for kids who are especially interested.

The greatest tribute the kids paid the stations was when they came into the room in the morning and asked me, "We got stations today?" and were disappointed when occasionally we did not. It was a system that made a hard morning's work into a pleasant and social experience and improved the kids' attitudes towards themselves and towards school. In better moments, I felt (in sharp contrast to my preoccupation with smaller classes my first year) that I could handle *more* kids in the room, perhaps as many as thirty, because it was so stable and having more kids would mean more people to help others and more personalities and ideas bouncing around the room.

However, there were many more days when I retracted this desire and was happy with what I had.

There are some serious questions to be raised by other teachers about the learning stations. Clearly those who tried to use the system would, as I did, adapt it to their own style of teaching and the constraints of their schools and nature of their students. But what of teachers with families, who cannot devote two hours to writing stations after school? What of teachers who are unable to spend eight or nine Saturdays during the year taking kids on field trips? What of teachers who are less facile at writing material than I was? And finally, what of beginning teachers? Could I have successfully implemented a learning-station program in my first year in the King School?

It seems to me that for those who believe in the benefits that come from this kind of program, ingenuity and teamwork can provide answers to all of these questions. Teachers who are short of time and hesitant about writing material might work in teams with other teachers in their own or nearby schools to pool their ideas and talents, delegating the job of writing to those more skilled at it, and sharing the material generated among all their classes. This kind of arrangement might reduce the burden of running the system to an hour-long meeting after school four days a week. As for field trips and some of the other time-consuming "frills" I added to the stations, I consider them important to getting to know the kids and winning their trust, but not integral to the success of the system. A teacher who knew kids better than I did or could use the time in school more effectively (or have shorter outings on weekday afternoons) might be able to dispense with these without damaging the station program. After all, the station time of the school day is open enough to offer many opportunities to talk to kids and get to know them.

As for beginning teachers, I am at odds with the conventional wisdom that they should "start tough," should try to imitate traditional authoritarian teaching with their first class, and then "loosen up" later. I feel that the learning-station classroom is a better starting point for new teachers, whatever methods they end up using. Asking teachers who are unsure of themselves and the kids and who haven't worked out their approach to teaching to try to dominate a class is a prescription for chaos and ulcers. A teacher-centered classroom has little intrinsic stability; it depends heavily on the personality of the teacher and creates difficult requirements of order and silence that the teacher must try to enforce. If the teacher is not sure of himself and his methods, he is going to be given precious little time to develop properly. Besides producing many harshly authoritarian teachers who are afraid to give kids any freedom and driving many other teachers out of schools, the first-year-teachers' trauma can be a complete waste of a year for a group of kids.

Starting with learning stations might get around some of the problems of the first year if the beginning teacher got support and materials from other teachers. A station type classroom well-stocked with materials and other activities has much more internal stability than a conventional classroom, so a teacher beginning with this setup might have more time to get to know the kids individually and work out a style of dealing with them. In a more stable decentralized classroom, new teachers might evolve their own ideas of how a class should be run and gradually implement them as they gained confidence and skill. There would still be many crises and embarrassing incidents and many bad days, but it would probably be a lot better than my first year.

But at the moment practically no education programs in colleges even begin to prepare new teachers for what they are getting into or equip them with a strategy for dealing with it. Preparation for teaching in ghetto schools is the least adequate, and yet many teachers begin their careers in such schools. It is indeed unfortunate that urban schools, where students already have so many handicaps, should have increasingly become the training ground for many new teachers, who then move out of the central city to more comfortable schools and put in their best years there.

Perhaps the learning stations (and other more open

classroom systems) provide a way out of this situation. An unstructured classroom can handle visitors and helpers because they do not put the "spell" of an authoritarian teacher in jeopardy; it can also handle student teachers and give them a much more active role than might be possible much of the time in more conventional classes. Walking around the room helping and talking to kids and practicing writing worksheets and correcting them with the master teacher, a student teacher might come very close to the actual role of the teacher and gain invaluable experience — if his education school would give him enough time in the classroom. This means (as Larry Cuban suggested in "Teacher and Community" in the *Harvard Educational Review,* Vol. 39, No. 2, Spring, 1969) turning most teacher-training programs completely around, from teaching "methods" and theory in their own classrooms to getting student teachers into real classrooms most of the time and *then* forming theories and generalizations from what they see and experience in them. Such a program of experience and induction, in conjunction with training in curriculum writing and a program of putting together teams of like-minded and compatible teachers within schools and cities, might begin to turn out teachers who were truly qualified to teach. Such a program would provide an opportunity for young teachers to work out their own style of teaching and develop some competence before they took over full responsibility for a classroom.

The orientation of most school systems in selecting teachers produces distortions similar to those of education schools in training them. The requirements for incoming teachers should change so that they focus less on academic credentials and theoretical expertise and more on this kind of on-the-spot training. Most school systems also have a lot to learn from North Dakota, where an intensive four-month in-service program has converted many experienced teachers to new methods.

The learning station system is not an idea limited either to the King School or the sixth grade. Many variations of it are in operation around the country and in England at many different grade levels. But clearly different ages of kids have different requirements. How does this system fit into a kindergarten-to-college scenario of educational reform? Here are my ideas.

Kids in the primary grades should have Leicestershire-type open classrooms, as they do in many parts of the country now. These would be very game- and toy-oriented in the early grades, and then gradually become more academically and book-oriented, with more paper work (as in my class) by the fifth grade. The "joy of learning" and freedom with responsibility should be the watchwords in these elementary classrooms, with a gradually increasing degree of responsibility to do things and get organized without direct supervision.

When they reach junior high school, kids need more specialized academic attention and should therefore be taught by teams of four or five teachers with different specialties in clusters or "mini-schools" within larger schools. The teachers in each team would work closely together to produce an integrated, interrelated curriculum, which could either be taught in the conventional junior-high-school format of kids moving from teacher to teacher, or, if greater stability was required, in homeroom with each teacher staying with one class and gathering materials and ideas from his colleagues in the other subject areas. Learning station-type classrooms would be possible in either arrangement, particularly if kids were given an uninterrupted double or triple period with one or two teachers and a number of stations in different areas. A portion of each day might be devoted to a "family group" meeting between small groups of kids and a teacher — a sort of expanded homeroom period with more chance to discuss problems and ideas from the day or of a nonacademic nature. These mini-schools might also operate in one large room on the "open space" concept, with teachers and resource people scattered around the room and perhaps modular scheduling.

In high school the boundaries of the school would disappear. The kids would increasingly be working or apprenticing at jobs in the city or community and reporting back to the school and meeting there for discussions and seminars on what it all means in terms of History, Science, Economics, Math, and English. This is the idea of the Parkways School in Philadelphia, the "school without walls," although it may need to be made more flexible to allow students who want to pursue purely academic subjects the opportunity to do so. Colleges that received kids with this kind of preparation would be dealing with people who were considerably more mature and experienced than those they admit now, and would doubtless have to make a number of changes in their curricula toward applying the academic learning to the real world. Many changes in this direction have already begun in some colleges, as they have at every level I have mentioned. They would certainly have more impact on the kids if they flowed from one level to another with the same basic objectives and themes.

Nine.

Conclusion

One day in December of my second year, a dejected colleague and I were talking about the way the kids charge up the stairs every morning the second after the bell rings to open school, racing to get to their classrooms. "Why are they in such a hurry?" he wondered. "They know what's up there." Yet I later discovered that he had missed the point. They do know what's up there: friends, fun, excitement, watching teachers winning and losing familiar battles, fire alarms, crises, fights, love affairs, and — occasionally — academic learning. In short, the secret of the kids in the King School (and the liberals will be the last ones to find this out) is that they love school. It's a gas. It's where all the action is and most of them wouldn't be anyplace else.

But while the kids have found ways to have a ball in school despite the school's wishes to the contrary, some would say that they are already "dead," that their personalities are permanently scarred and twisted by their experiences in the public schools. These critics say that the schools are keeping kids down by not preparing them for a competitive society, and thus *are* preparing them for their "places" in a racist society. According to them, the kids' enjoyment of school is laughter on a sinking ship.

Teachers who agree with this indictment have tended to avoid or drop out of the public schools; they see change within them as virtually impossible, and feel that by teaching in them they would be helping to prop up institutions whose downfall would be a boon to education. Some of these people have gone on to establish or teach in alternative schools outside the public school systems. A few have stayed in the system but see themselves as saboteurs, throwing wrenches into the machinery and organizing students and parents to bring the system closer to breakdown and then, they hope, to a new and better order.

My reaction to this indictment of the public schools has been somewhat different. It is certainly shaped by the fact that I happened to get a job in the Boston public schools and was fortunate in terms of the ideas and support I got from other people to become a successful teacher within them. But I think it a questionable premise to expect the downfall of the public schools or to think that alternative schools will ever have much impact on the systems and educate more than a handful of fortunate kids.

I also think it is misleading to make the same kind of moral argument about a teacher's participation in an admittedly faulted school system that radicals have made about the people working on war policies in the Pentagon. This argument misses the point that school systems are extraordinarily decentralized, that the job of each little cog in the machine is what the whole system is all about. With tact and a little luck, a good teacher can do a great deal with a group of kids, and the experiences which that teacher has with those kids are for keeps, and can't be taken away. Given this, it makes sense to try to teach kids and influence other teachers in schools where most of the kids and the basic resources already are. Then one can only hope that some momentum will build up behind new teaching ideas and that stimulating, happy classrooms will multiply.

Besides disagreeing with a moral indictment of the public schools, I have also come to disagree with the idea that the kids are "dead." When I first began to teach in the King School, I was influenced by this notion and approached the kids with a certain amount of liberal pity. Over the last three years I have found that these kids don't need or want pity — there is nothing pathetic in their fierce independence, flashing intuition, and hard-won ability to deal with a very tough environment. The students I have taught came through schools that supposedly destroyed their hearts and minds. Yet here they are, full of life, their hearts and minds belonging only to them, every one of them yearning, reaching out to be someone. Instead of weakness and defeat, I have found toughness and vitality. Far from being "dead," I have found them eager and full of potential, endearingly alive, and perhaps better able to cope with many aspects of life than more "fortunate" kids.

But I *can* see how the kids' environment and experiences in public schools have built up a very effective resistance to conventional teaching by conventional teachers with conventional materials, making success with these methods and materials an act of genius — and there is a chronic shortage of geniuses. I can see how the kids have developed a style (some would say a culture) of coolness and toughness which protects them from the hard edges of their environment and helps them feel better about themselves, while the school spends much of its time trying to *undo* that style and remake the kids in its own image. Both see their integrity as being at stake — most of the kids are not about to be remade, while the school insists that it can't do its job of teaching until there is "discipline" on its own terms — and the stage is set for the kind of conflict that racks so many public schools. But in the ensuing struggle for order in the school, the kids hold nearly all the advantages (especially with the abolition of corporal punishment and the growing awareness of legal procedures in the black community), and victory for the school over the antics of the kids, usually in the form of silence in a classroom or an assembly, is a purely neutral educational accomplishment. At that point the kids have usually retired deep into shells of self-protection and fantasy.

So while the kids have the ability and the desire to learn and the school sincerely wants to teach them, there is little effective preparation, academic or otherwise, for the rigors of high schools, colleges, and the job market. While they are far from "dead" now, I can see how many kids in the King School may have a "death sentence" in American society. Unemployment, drugs, and crime all lurk ahead.

There has been a lot of writing about the effects of these violent forces in the black community on kids' performance in school, and some speculation about how much better ghetto kids would do in school if they didn't have to live in ghettos and worry about all these things. But how can you say this to an individual child? What does it mean to him? The eradication of the *causes* of violence in the ghettos — poverty, racism, unemployment — will not come in his lifetime. What will happen to the generations of kids in the meantime? Will schools like the King continue to turn off the kids and thus encourage them to turn on themselves, the schools, and the society with even greater violence?

It is true that most ghetto kids find it difficult to get involved in learning in their public schools and don't do as well as their white, middle-class counterparts. But is this entirely their fault? Can *they* change their communities or America and make themselves into nice, well-behaved children, who are willing to sit in quiet rows and listen to their teachers? The school often talks to the kids as though they could and should; it is a position I took many times my first year, when I was unable to cope with their energy. But it is crazy to think this way. You can't order kids to stop being the people they are. (You can try to brainwash them that they are supposed to act a certain way, but they have ways of dealing with that too.) Trying to remake them hardly helps them feel more confident in what they are and ready to learn and develop into what they might become. Nor does it help them deal with the environment into which they were born.

Some of what the kids are is delightful and full of promise. Some of it is troubled and violent. But they can't change themselves overnight or deny what they are. Neither can the school. Rather *it is the school that must change* if the kids are to become self-confident and fulfill their potential. The school must accept the kids for what they are and stop denying that they have problems or trying to keep the problems out of "disciplined" classrooms. The school must find ways of presenting learning in such a way that kids can get involved without being made to feel that they are failures or that they are in some way sissies and teachers' pets. The school must find ways to help work out the fantasies and violent realities of the kids' lives so they aren't haunted or diminished by them. It is only when the school accepts the kids and the community as they are and stops trying to varnish them with its textbook notion of how they ought to be, that the kids will let themselves be touched and taught by it. And it is only then that the "death sentence" hanging over the kids can be put on appeal — or perhaps lifted.

Sensitive and sympathetic teachers and administrators (of whatever color) are the first step. More open classroom formats like the learning stations are the second step. And community control (in conjunction with a metropolitan school board to distribute funds, set general standards, and achieve economies of scale) may be the third. Whatever the method, schools like the King must create a climate where the kids' dynamism — so much of it expressed in negative, self-destructive ways now because of the position the school takes — can express itself in positive ways that will contribute to dealing with the problems of the community and to their own development.

No one has hard facts and figures to prove that this general approach and the specific ideas put forward in this book really produce results; at this point there is only subjective evidence. But I hope the facts and figures (for those who want them) are not far off, and that such ideas will be developed and slowly spread through public schools by a process of demonstration and persuasion. One reason for optimism, and the thing that impressed me most last year, is the degree to which kids, parents, and many school administrators are ready for new ideas. More and more people have come to think that the authoritarian, teacher-dominated classroom, even when it works without disruption, is just not producing well-educated or well-adjusted kids. The totally unstructured classroom is also somewhat discredited by what many parents and schools see as its lack of purpose and direction. But a compromise such as the learning stations may find a surprising amount of support. It certainly has in my case.

The question remains: will the King School break with its own history and do more than respond to rising chaos with grudging concessions and innovations? Will it seize an idea or follow a personality and work to solve the problems of the kids and the community before they destroy it? At the moment these are open questions.

In a broader sense, perhaps it is naïve to think that revolutionizing classroom teaching or approaching students with a different attitude in the public schools will give the kids a better grasp of the basic skills, or (if they grasp the skills they need) that they will be any better off in high schools and colleges, or (if they do better there) that the job market will accept them or even have room for them. Looking at things this way can be discouraging. There is so much work to be done at so many levels; schools are the lowest and most microcosmic level, and even the best work there can easily be demolished later on. There are even those who argue that it isn't worth giving kids a really good year because it raises their hopes falsely and makes the realities of their lives in America that much harder to bear.

I don't agree with this approach. Without a beginning, without hope, schools will never change and will never prepare kids to live in or change this country. Certainly schools will not be turned around by bitter and hardened kids without a vision of what classrooms and schools can be. Most of the kids I taught in 6-G and 6-D have a great feeling about the year they spent in our classroom. In it they enjoyed reading, enjoyed doing Math, enjoyed writing stories, enjoyed typing things, enjoyed playing games, enjoyed discussing things with each other and with me, and above all enjoyed doing well and feeling competent. These experiences are permanent and will stay in their minds waiting for other teachers or classrooms which turn them on in the same way. They may be bitter when other teachers don't meet their new expectations, but not much more bitter than they would

have been without being in our classroom. Besides, the kids will have specific ideas on what makes a classroom fun, and some of them (and their parents) may become very effective partisans for innovation as they move up through their schools.

While what I am doing may seem absurdly small, while the inkblot of innovation that will spread upward from my classes may affect only a small number of kids and an even smaller number of teachers, I can't see quitting. And when I think of another class next year — the new faces and the new ideas I want to use — I can push aside such thoughts for a while and plunge in while America makes up its mind whether it can and will give these kids a chance.

APPENDIXES

The following lists give a rough idea of what I covered in the station worksheets in the course of the 1971-72 school year. I took the Math and English topics from the Boston curriculum guide and broke them down into bite-sized chunks (or units), which could be covered in about four days of stations. The Spelling words came from a list "officially" designated as words that sixth-graders should know, from subjects that came up in class and other worksheets, and from my own searches through the dictionary for interesting and useful words. The Social Studies curriculum, perhaps the least well-developed, emerged over three years from my own ideas and those of a few colleagues in the school, as did the Creative Writing topics and the ideas used in the General station. The choice of the Reading topic was always a last-minute decision, with a number of perennially interesting topics vying with exciting current events.

The sample learning-station worksheets after the curriculum lists give an idea of my own techniques for presenting ideas and squeezing them onto a small, self-explanatory page. The sheets are certainly not as polished as any published classroom material, but then they are not as dull either; at least they have advantages of freshness, relevance to the interests of the class, using names and incidents from the class, and following themes from subject to subject and day to day, which textbooks will never have. In addition, the sheets gave my classes a balance between academic rigor and less heavy games and puzzles, helped the kids learn how to work on their own, and prepared them for certain kinds of I.Q. tests that would otherwise have been loaded against them.

Writing this kind of material is a knack which it took me several months to acquire. After two years of writing learning-station worksheets, I still occasionally step outside the written rapport that has developed between me and the kids and produce a dud — something that is too heavy, too hard or easy, or just not interesting. This seems to happen most often when I start taking a worksheet too seriously — rewriting it and trying to put too much into it — or when I prepare material too far in advance. The essence of writing this kind of worksheet seems to lie in finding ideas, approaches, gimmicks, games, and topics that are appealing to a particular class and then writing the worksheets quickly and, if possible, humorously, the night before they are going to be used.

For two years I have wished my school would schedule free time each day, when several like-minded colleagues and I could sit down and write such materials as a group. (Doing this after school is out of the question because everyone is too exhausted.) The results of this kind of group process would probably be much stronger than mine, since the worksheets produced would draw on more experience and insight. Such a group of teachers might use its meetings to drum up ideas and then delegate the job of writing the worksheets to members who were good in certain areas — the group might develop a specialist in each subject area and have someone who could do the graphics and illustrations well. This way, each class that used copies of the worksheets would benefit from the diversity and specialization of a number of teachers while still having the stability of being with one homeroom teacher most of the time. For the teachers, this process would undoubtedly be good for morale, increase the awareness of everyone in the group to different approaches and techniques, and would cut down the work load.

A. Mathematics Curriculum

1. Fifth-grade review
2. Averaging
3. Writing numbers as words
4. Place value and decimals
5. Decimals — addition and subtraction
6. Decimals — one-number multiplication
7. Decimals — one-number division
8. Two-number multiplication
9. Two-number division
10. Decimals — two-number multiplication and division
11. The names of parts in addition, subtraction, multiplication, and division
12. Factors and primes
13. Prime factors
14. Ratio and proportion
15. Weights, measures, time, and money
16. Fractions: introduction and addition and subtraction of like denominators
17. Fractions — topheavy and mixed
18. Fractions — addition and subtraction with unlike denominators
19. Fractions — Canceling and multiplication
20. Fractions — division
21. Percent — introduction and from decimals

B. English Curriculum

1. Declarative, interrogative, imperative, and exclamatory sentences
2. Punctuation — quotation marks
3. Punctuation — apostrophes
4. Punctuation — commas
5. Punctuation — colons and semicolons
6. Synonyms, antonyms, and homonyms
7. Phonics and word-attack skills
8. Capitalizing
9. Dividing up sentences and paragraphs
10. Subject and predicate
11. Nouns and verbs
12. Pronouns
13. Adjectives and adverbs
14. Prepositions, conjunctions, and interjections
15. All parts of speech together
16. Proper and improper nouns
17. Tenses of verbs
18. Agreement of verbs
19. Alphabetizing and syllabificating
20. Prefixes and suffixes
21. Business letters
22. Commonly confused homonyms

C. Social Studies Curriculum

1. Directions on a map of the classroom
2. Freehand drawing of a map of the classroom
3. Map of the school and immediate surroundings
4. Map of the neighborhood — streets and features
5. Map of Boston — neighborhoods, parks, rivers, airport, etc.
6. Map of the United States — identification of major states, cities, lakes, oceans, etc.
7. Map of the world — identification of major continents, oceans, geographic features
8. Black history — geography and peoples of Africa
9. Black history — slavery
10. Black history — the Civil Rights movement
11. Black history — Martin Luther King
12. Black history — Malcolm X
13. The modern city — comparison with the ancient city
14. The modern city — pollution
15. The modern city — transportation
16. The modern city — race relations
17. The modern city — education
18. Greek myths and their meanings — modern scientific explanations of the same things
19. The reasons for laws — inductive unit on why some major laws were made

20. The history of the 60s
21. China — peoples and history
22. Religions
23. The history of the King School
24. Current events

D. Some General Station Activities

Crossword puzzles

Secret codes

Gouping exercises

Exercises in following directions

Slang into formal English

The five senses and their uses

Values and priorities in the class

Fact versus opinion

Elephant and other jokes

Family trees and relationships

A problems column: answering letters of distress

Questions on the lyrics of rock songs

Brain teasers

Nonverbal Math problems

Moral dilemmas

Mazes and puzzles

Current events issues

Unscrambling words and sentences

Making graphs

Miscellaneous drawings, lists, resolutions, and class
organization

E. Some Reading Station Topics

The Pentagon Papers
The Alaska Pipeline
The Manchurian Candidate
The Loneliness of the Long Distance Runner
The Birth of Bangla Desh
Bobby Fischer
Cat's Cradle
The Spanish Bullfight
The Radar Systems of Bats
The Marin Courthouse Escape Attempt
Satchel Paige and the Hall of Fame
The Story of Muhammad Ali
The Ali-Frazier Fight
The Death of Whitney Young
Agnew's Visit to Boston
California Earthquakes
The Manson Murders
Heroin (a four-part series)
Love Story
Charade
The Plague in Denver
American Ping-Pong Team in China
A Night to Remember
Maurice Gordon, Boston Landlord

*Plots of movies

The Wrong-Way Bus Lane Idea
South Africa
The Story of Dwight Johnson
The Atomic Bomb
The Bermuda Triangle
The War of the Worlds
Tanker Collision at San Francisco
Naomi, a Nigerian Girl
The Fox of Chicago
Herbert Wirth, Famous Peddler
German Submarine off the Florida Coast
Mutiny on the Bounty (two parts)
Doctor Delano Meriwether
Dan Buster's Gold
The My Lai Massacre
The Death of the SST
Mount Etna's Eruptions
Baby Seals in Canada
Sickle-Cell Anemia
Sign Language and Chimpanzees
Attica State Prison
East Boston versus Logan Airport
Botulism
The Story of George Jackson
Freedom Foods, Black Supermarket
The King of Hearts
Sacco and Vanzetti
The Kennedy Assassination
Dr. Strangelove

*Plots of movies

F. A Ten-Word, One-Week Spelling Unit

Monday: Copy ten new words with part of speech, meaning, and a sentence into spelling dictionaries in loose-leaf binders.

Tuesday: Put the ten words into blank spaces in sentences and into spaces by their definitions.

Wednesday: Use each word in an original sentence that shows that you know what it means (referring to spelling dictionaries if necessary).

Thursday: Find the ten words (and ten other words) in a puzzle and write them down below.

Friday: Test. Write the ten words and their definitions from oral pronunciation by teacher.

G. Creative Writing Topics
(Used During the School Year 1970-71)

— Write a story, true or make-believe, about a time when you have been very frightened (scared).

— Pretend you are writing a letter to a friend in another country about this school. Tell them all about it, good things and bad things — the kids, your friends, teachers, food, gym, and so on.

— Write a letter to President Nixon telling him what is wrong with the country and what he can do to make things better. You might talk about Vietnam, bad schools, prejudice, crime, drugs, pollution, and other things.

— Write about two things: times you have been sad and times you have been happy.

— Write a story about times you have been very *angry*.

— Write a story about dreams you have had.

— Write a list of your favorite things.

— Write a story about the things you *hear, see,* and *smell* on your street every day.

— Write a story about the kind of apartment or house you would like to live in. Tell *all* about it.

— One day I was walking down the street when suddenly I heard a loud screech of tires. (Finish the story.)

— Write about what the weather is like in the fall (right now), how things look, and how it makes you feel.

— Write about what it would be like to go to jail for nine months. Fill all the lines with how you would feel, what you would think about, and how you would feel when you got out.

— Write about love.

— Write about the weather this morning — tell how it makes things look, smell, sound — and how it makes you feel.

— Write a make-believe (or real) story about what it would be like to wake up in the middle of the night and find your house was on fire.

— Write a story or poem about what it would be like to be an animal or a bird. You can choose what you want to be.

— If you were principal of the King School, what would you do to change it?

— Write about snow.

— Pretend you had just made friends with someone who was *blind.* You would have to tell your friend what everything looked like because they couldn't see it. Write how you would describe these things to your friend: your face; our classroom; your house; the leaves in fall; a beautiful cold day.

— Write what you think about drugs and the drug problem. It would be a good idea if you told about people you know or things you have heard or seen. Why do people take drugs? How can we stop them? Should we stop them?

— Describe the storm on Wednesday night and Thursday. How did it make you feel? How did it make things look?

— Pretend you are a sports writer in a newspaper.

Write what you think is going to happen in the fight between Ali and Frazier.

— Write what you think it is like to die. If you want to, you can make a story up, like about a car accident or a gunfight. Try to think what would go through your mind as it happens.

— Write about the thing you most want to do right now. It can be anything. Tell why you want to do it.

— Write about what you think the U.S.A. will be like in fifty years. Think about all the new inventions, and also the problems we may have.

— Say what it means to you to be black.

— Write a story or a poem about rain.

— Write about what it would be like to have only one leg. What would you *not* be able to do? Would there be any advantages?

— Write about what it would be like to be a policeman.

— See if you can write a full description of what happened in school yesterday. Be like a reporter — remember important things inside the class and outside it. Say how you felt about things.

— Write what the different colors mean to you: red is . . . , green is . . . , blue, yellow, pink, gold, black, white, silver.

— What would it be like to be a heroin addict? Make up a whole story about it. Would you get off the drug? What would your family think? How would you get money for the drug? Would you be able to work?

— Describe the gerbil and the way it lives. What does it eat? What is the cage like? What does it look like? What does it do? What does it think of us? What did it think when its friend died? Shall we give it a name?

— Write a poem or a story about spring and the way it makes you feel.

— Choose one person in the room. Write everything you know about them. Write about the good things. Write the bad things. What do they look like? What do they talk like? What do they act like? Why do you like them? It can be any person, including me.

— Tell about animals you like and don't like.

— If you could turn into a fly and go anywhere you wanted without being noticed by people, what places would you go and what would you want to see and listen to?

— Write about the things you hate most. It can be a list, a story, or a poem.

— Pretend you were a very popular person, like one of the Jackson 5. What would be the good things and the bad things about being very popular?

— Describe how these things would *feel* to you: (1) putting an ice cube up to your lips; (2) petting a furry cat; (3) combing your hair; (4) crumpling up a piece of paper; (5) biting into an apple.

— Make up a story about a boy or girl your age who runs away from home. Try to make it a long story with lots of things happening to them. You can have it end any way you like.

— Make up a story about what you would do if you went into your bedroom and found a person from another planet sitting on your bed.

— Write about what it would be like to be an elephant.

— Write a story, true or make-believe, that uses these words: police, drugs, hospital, autopsy, accident, operation, family, funeral, church, gang, teenagers, girl friend, Cadillac.

— Write about what you would most like to do over the Christmas vacation.

— Remember the Charlie Brown book *Happiness Is a*

Warm Puppy? We are going to try to write some things like that today. I will start you off: School is . . . Home is . . . Happiness is . . . Love is . . . Anger is . . . Fear is . . .

— Pretend you had a lot of money. Write about the things you would give your family and friends for Christmas.

— Write a long story about a snowball fight where one kid gets very seriously hurt, maybe killed.

— Write about Santa Claus. Tell the story of what he is supposed to do. Do you believe in him? Did you used to when you were small?

— Write a story about what it would be like to be snowed into the King School for two weeks. There is a huge blizzard during school and no one can leave. What would people do? Where would they sleep? How would you feel?

— Tell me about what happened to you and what you did over the Christmas vacation. What did you see on TV? What did you do when it snowed? What did you get as presents? Who did you see? What did you think? How did you feel?

— Make up a story using these words: Vietnam, bullet, guerrilla, jungle, snake, tiger, helicopter, soldiers, enemy, river, battle, death.

— Write a composition about what Martin Luther King means to you.

— (Analysis, for a number of days, of paintings on the wall.)

— Tell me how the class was different yesterday when I was gone.

— Think of one thing, good or bad, that happened to you over the vacation. Write about it. Try to tell all about it and fill all the lines.

— How do you think the class is going? We have about two months of school left. What should we do before then? What shall we change?

— If you were Superman (you could fly, see through walls, and were very strong), what would you do? How would you use your powers?

— It was a sunny Saturday afternoon and I was sitting out front talking to a friend. (Finish the story.)

— Look at the pictures on the board. Then write what it would be like to live in China.

— Write about what it would be like to take a very long trip across the ocean in a little boat all by yourself.

— Write the way you feel about sleep.

— Write about your favorite sport (basketball, baseball, hockey, football, running, rowing, tennis, high jumping, pole vaulting, soccer, or anything else). Tell about the people you have heard about who play this sport, and why you like it. Tell about things you have heard have happened in this sport.

— Write about the Vietnam War.

— (Descriptions of parts of the body shown in highly magnified *Life* pictures.)

— (Descriptions of various machines at a bread factory we visited.)

— Write about what it would be like if you couldn't talk for a whole week. How would you communicate with people? What would you not be able to do? Would you like it?

— Write what you think of the Black Muslim religion after listening to Minister George X yesterday.

— Describe the kind of neighborhood you would like to live in. Tell about the houses, and people, and the other things you would like it to have. Draw pictures if you like.

— Write about teachers you have had who have made you feel cheap.

— If you were listening to a radio and you heard that the Russians were attacking and you had one day before the end of the world, what would you do?

— Who do you like best, Malcolm X or Martin Luther
King? Why?

— How did you like the stations this year? What do
you think I should do differently next year?

H. Some Sample Worksheets

September 13, 1971

SOCIAL STUDIES STATION

Name: _____

Here is a map of this classroom, looking from above. ⟶

Here are the directions:

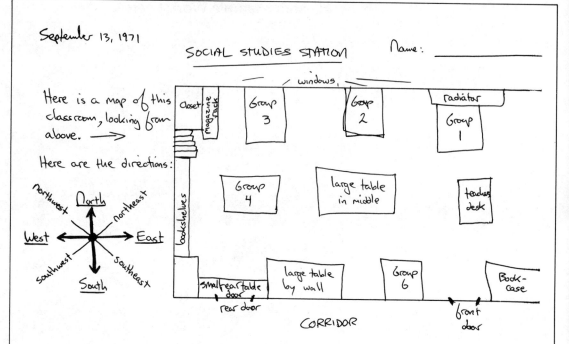

Now give the direction from the first place to the second place:

FROM	TO	DIRECTION
Group 4 ------------------------	large table in middle -----	_____
Group 6 ------------------------	teacher's desk -----------	_____
bookcase ----------------------	Group 6 ------------------	_____
small table by rear door ------	Group 4 ------------------	_____
closet ------------------------	bookcase -----------------	_____
magazine rack ------------------	closet --------------------	_____
large table by wall -----------	large table in middle ----	_____
teacher's desk ----------------	Group 1 ------------------	_____
Group 2 -----------------------	rear door ----------------	_____
Group 6 -----------------------	Group 3 ------------------	_____

*** What is the opposite direction of: North _____ East _____

Southwest _____ Northwest _____ South _____

Northeast _____ West _____

210

October 27, 1971   <u>SOCIAL STUDIES STATION</u   Name:_____

Get out the map of the neighborhoods of Boston from yesterday.
Remember that the different neighborhoods are in red.

1. What neighborhood is just north of Franklin Park?_____

2. What neighborhood is to the west of Roslindale?_____

3. What neighborhood is to the west of Allston?_____

4. What neighborhood is to the north of Beacon Hill?_____

5. What neighborhood is to the north, across the Charles River, from Beacon Hill?

                                                     _____

6. What city sticks into Boston from the west?_____

7. What neighborhood goes farthest to the north?_____

8. In what neighborhood are there the most tall buildings? (Guess.) _____

9. What direction is it from the King School to Franklin Field? _____

10. If you wanted to go from Mattapan Square to the Prudential Center by <u>boat</u>, how
    would you do it? (Give directions)

   _____

   _____

   _____

11. Look at the runways at the airport.
    Planes always have to take off <u>going into the wind</u>. Otherwise they might get
    blown to one side or not get off the ground in time.
    Look at the plane on one of the runways. Can you tell from that plane which way
    the wind was blowing when the map was drawn?_____

12. Which way is the wind blowing when the planes take off over the King School?

   _____

13. See if you can find out the answers to these questions:

    1. In what neighborhood of Boston do the most black people live?_____

    2. In what neighborhood do the most Irish people live?_____

    3. In what neighborhood do the most Italian people live?_____

    4. In what neighborhood do the most rich white people live?_____

    5. In what neighborhood do the most Chinese people live?_____

    6. In what neighborhood do the most college students live?_____

    7. In what neighborhood do the most Jewish people live?_____

November 17, 1971   SOCIAL STUDIES STATION   Name:_____

Look at your maps from yesterday's Social Studies station:

1. What continent are we on? _____

2. What continent is just south of our continent? _____

3. Can you find out from the globe or the map what the name of the canal is that
   makes a short cut between North and South America? (Hint: it would be dug
   in the narrowest place between the two continents.)

                                              _____

4. What is the name of the ocean between North America and Europe?_____

5. What is the name of the large island next to North America and very close to
   the North Pole? _____

6. What is the name of the large land mass at the South Pole? _____

7. What is the smallest continent? (Here are the continents: Europe, Asia, North
   America, South America, Antarctica, Australia, Africa.)

                                              _____

8. Name the continents that touch the equator. _____

   _____

9. What continent is Vietnam in? _____

10. Which is the biggest ocean? (Here are the oceans: Atlantic, Pacific, Indian, Arctic.)

   _____

11. Which continent do you think would be the coldest? _____
    Why? _____

12. Which continent do you think would be the hottest? _____ Why? _____

    _____

13. Which is the biggest continent? _____

14. When it is day in Boston, it is _____ in Vietnam.
    Tell why this is true. _____

    _____

15. If you wanted to take the fastest route from Boston to Vietnam (God forbid!),
    would you go around the world to the east or to the west? _____

16. Name one country in each continent: North America: _____

    South America: _____   Europe: _____   Asia: _____

    Africa: _____   (The reason I didn't include Australia is that
    it is one country. The reason I didn't include Antarctica is that hardly
    anyone lives there because it is all ice and snow.)

November 29, 1971   SOCIAL STUDIES STATION   Name - _____

The Ancient and the Modern City

The modern city, like Boston and New York, has a lot of problems. We will
spend most of this week talking about them in this station.

But today I want to get you thinking about how the modern city is different
from the kind of city that men lived in a long, long time ago in ancient Greece
or Rome or some other country in Europe or Asia when civilization was just
getting started. We have a lot of inventions like cars and televisions and so
forth that make our cities a lot different from theirs.

This is a real test of your imagination. Can you think what ancient people
did to fulfill the same needs as these things do for us:

THIS IS WHAT WE USE | WHAT DID ANCIENT PEOPLE DO TO GET THE SAME THING?

1. cars, buses, subways, planes _____

2. movies and television _____

3. newspapers _____

4. supermarkets _____

5. underground sewer pipes _____

6. radiators heating houses _____

7. hospitals _____

8. antidotes for diseases _____

9. electric lights _____

10. nuclear bombs _____

** For extra credit, you can either draw a picture or write a story in your
   Creative Writing book about what it would be like to live in an ancient city.

December 2, 1971   SOCIAL STUDIES STATION   Name: _____

* MORE on POLLUTION *

① A man has to go to work every day. His job is 2 miles from
where he lives. It is <u>easiest</u> for him to drive his car to work.
But he hears that driving a car makes the city's pollution worse,
and pollution is bad for everyone, especially old people and babies.
Should he take the bus? Should he ride a bicycle? Say why.

FILL
ALL
THE
LINES
→

_____

_____

_____

_____

_____

_____

_____

② A small town has a paper factory. All the men in the town work
in the factory and make enough money to stay alive. There are no
other jobs in the town.   Then the government tells the factory
that it is polluting the air and the water badly. The factory tries
to stop the pollution, but it doesn't have enough money to stop it.
The town has a <u>choice</u>: should it close the factory and put all
the men on welfare? Or should it keep the factory going, keep the
men working, and forget about the pollution?

FILL
'EM
UP

_____

_____

_____

_____

_____

_____

214

December 14, 1971   SOCIAL STUDIES STATION   Name:_____ ----

Today we are beginning a unit on LAWS.

The point of this unit is to make you think about <u>why</u> we have laws.
We are going to do this by having you make up a bunch of laws yourself.

PRETEND THERE WERE NO LAWS IN THE WORLD.

PEOPLE BEING WHAT THEY ARE, BAD THINGS WOULD HAPPEN.

IT IS UP TO YOU TO MAKE RULES THAT PEOPLE CAN FOLLOW TO MAKE THINGS SAFE AND PEACEFUL.

Here are some unfair situations. Make <u>general</u> rules to stop things like that from happening.

Situation 1

A man spends a lot of time and effort building a house to live in.
When he finishes another man comes with a gun and forces the man who
built the house to move out. The man with the gun moves in and lives there.

WHAT RULE WOULD YOU MAKE TO STOP THIS KIND OF THING FROM HAPPENING?

_____

_____

_____

Situation 2

A President doesn't like people telling him he is wrong. A man criticizes
him and he throws the man in jail for the rest of his life without a trial.

WHAT RULE WOULD YOU MAKE TO STOP THIS KIND OF THING FROM HAPPENING?

_____

_____

_____

Situation 3

A man invents a cure for cancer after working for 20 years in his laboratory.
Another man gets the idea from him and pretends that he invented it. The
man who stole the secret makes a million dollars by selling the cure.

WHAT LAW SHOULD BE MADE TO PREVENT THIS?

_____

_____

_____

Situation 4

Two men get into an argument. One pulls a knife and kills the other.

WHAT LAW SHOULD BE MADE? _____

Mount Etna is at it again

Off the coast of Italy there is an island called Sicily. On the island of Sicily there is a large mountain called Mount Etna. But this is not just an ordinary mountain. It is a sleeping volcano which every once in a while wakes up and erupts.

When a volcano erupts, it spills red hot rock all over the countryside, and burns everything below it to a crisp. There is nothing you can do about it but run away. The red hot rock is just like water, and runs down the valleys, burning trees and grass and houses and animals that haven't had the sense to get out of the way.

The lava that comes out of a volcano comes from the inside of the Earth. Usually the center of the Earth, which is all red hot rock, stays inside and doesn't bother the outside of the Earth, which is quite cool. But every once in a while a crack develops in the rocks between the inside and the outisde of the Earth. This can happen when there is an earthquake. It could even happen if there were a large enough bomb dropped on one part of the Earth.

When a crack develops, the lava flows from the center of the Earth and out of a volcano like Mount Etna.

Mount Etna has not erupted many times. People felt safe in living quite near it, thinking that it would not erupt all over them. Many years ago it did erupt, and the people of a village nearby saw that the lava was going to run through their town and destroy it. So all of the people in the village went to the ocean and prayed to God that their village would be spared. When they got back to the village they found that the lava had turned aside and the village was spared. They were sure that their prayers had been answered.

Last May, Mount Etna bagan to erupt again. It shot pieces of rock and lava into the air, and a huge river of lava began to flow down the side of the mountain towards the same town. The people in the village saw what was going to happen, and once again they went to the ocean and prayed to God that their village would not be destroyed. Some people thought God was punishing them for the things they had done wrong. They prayed for forgiveness and promised to be good. And once again the lava did not destroy their village.

This week Mount Etna is at it again. It is smoking and rumbling and making strange noises. And the people are getting nervous again. We do not know what will happen this time.

QUESTIONS:

1. What island is Mount Etna on?_____

2. What is special about this mountain?

_____

_____

3. Why is lava from a volcano so dangerous?

_____

_____

4. Where does lava come from?

_____

5. What are two things that might let lava come to the surface of the Earth?

_____

_____

_____

6. Why do people live anywhere near it?

_____

_____

7. What do the people in the village do when they see the volcano erupting?

_____

_____

8. In your opinion, were the people's prayers answered by God, or was it just good luck that their village was saved?

_____

_____

9. What did some people think God was doing by having the volcano erupt?

_____

10. Why are the people of the village nervous this week?

September 14, 1971

<u>GENERAL STATION</u>

Name;_____

Every person who is not handicapped (blind, deaf, dumb, etc) has five senses.
They are: hearing, seeing, feeling, smelling, and tasting.
These are are the ways we find out about what is going on around us. Without them,
we wouldn't know anything - we wouldn't really be alive.
Some people say there is a <u>sixth</u> sense, which they call mental telepathy.
They say this is when you can tell something is about to happen or tell what
another person is thinking without using your five other senses. Other people
don't believe in this. Do you? _____

** Here is a list of things that might happen. On the line after each one, tell
which sense (there can be more than one) you would use to know about them.

1. the screech of a car's tires - _____

2. the sun - _____

3. hot water - _____

4. a poster - _____

5. dynamite exploding - _____

6. a bee biting you on your back - _____

7. a rotten egg - _____

8. a cloud - _____

9. a bakery down the street - _____

10. words printed in a book - _____

11. whether someone in another city is thinking about you - _____

12. an earthquake - _____

13. a loud band playing music in a small room - _____

14. whether a radiator is hot or cold - _____

15. a television show - _____

16. an apple pie - _____

17. pollution - _____

18. a person screaming - _____

19. whether a knife is sharp - _____

20. bad breath - _____

** Now turn the paper over and see if you can write what the five senses are.

217

Sept. 21, 1971　　　　GENERAL STATION　　　Name: _____

Put these things into six groups.
Then give each group a name.

the Beatles
guitar
seeing
great
the Supremes
enormous
Science
drums
Social Studies
hearing
Jackson Five
smelling
large
flute
Math.
Temptations
Spelling
bass fiddle
tasting
huge
Sly (and the Family Stone)
saxophone
touching
big
English

Group 1
① _____
② _____
③ _____
④ _____
⑤ _____
name: _____

Group 2
① _____
② _____
③ _____
④ _____
⑤ _____
name: _____

Group 3
① _____
② _____
③ _____
④ _____
⑤ _____
name: _____

Group 4
① _____
② _____
③ _____
④ _____
⑤ _____
name: _____

Group 5
① _____
② _____
③ _____
④ _____
⑤ _____
name: _____

Group 6
① _____
② _____
③ _____
④ _____
⑤ _____
name: _____

Sept. 21, 1971   MATH. STATION   Name: _____

To find the average: ① add everything up
                      ② divide by how many things there are.

① What is the average of 12, 3, 7, 2, and 1 ?   _____

② What is the average of 100, 365, and 3 ?   _____

③ What is the average of 9, 13, 12, and 2 ?   _____

④ What is the average of 16 and 38 ?   _____

⑤ What is the average of 9, 7, 2, 4, and 2 ?   _____

⑥ A man has 3 sons. One is 10, one is 8, and one is 6.
    What is their average age ?   _____

⑦ One boy is 3 feet and one is 5 feet tall. What is their
    average height ?   _____

⑧ A race car makes four turns around a track. the first time
    it takes 55 seconds, next 53, next 61, and next 51.
    What was the average time ?   _____

⑨ What is the average of 6, 8, 2, 9, 10, 11, 200, 5, 8, 50, and 21 ?

                                        _____

⑩ What is the average of 3 and 5 ?   _____

October 5, 1971   GENERAL STATION   Name: _____

Here is the difference between a fact and an opinion:

    a FACT is true and you can prove it

    an OPINION is up to the person who believes it - you can have an argument about it.

Tell whether these are fact or opinion:

1. Blue is the nicest color in the world. _____

2. The U.S.A. is made up of fifty states. _____

3. Richard Nixon is President of the U.S.A. _____

4. Richard Nixon is a bad President. _____

5. The Temptations sing beautifully. _____

6. The King School is located at the top of Lawrence Avenue in Roxbury. _____

7. The King School is the worst school in the city of Boston. _____

8. A dictionary is a place where you can find the meanings of words. _____

9. Black is beautiful. _____

10. White is beautiful. _____

11. Shaft is a fine movie. _____

12. There are about 800 students in the King School. _____

13. Math is fun. _____

14. Mr. Marshall is a handsome dude. _____

15. God created the earth and all that therein is. _____

16. When you die you will rise to heaven. _____

17. The school has had a number of false fire alarms this year. _____

18. Going outside for fire alarms is fun! _____

19. Kevin White has been a good Mayor of Boston. _____

20. We have Spanish second period Thursday. _____

Now try writing some facts and opinions of your own. Tell what each one is.

_____

_____

_____

_____

_____

220

October 19, 1971   <u>GENERAL STATION</u>   Name:_____

Open your binder to <u>Cloud Nine</u>, which was the fourth song we had.
If you didn't get it, come and ask me for a copy. Then answer these questions:

1. Where was the person in the song raised? _____

2. Did he live in a big house? _____ How do you know? _____

_____

3. Did he sleep alone? _____ How did he sleep?_____

4. Did his father have a job?_____ Why do you think so? Was it his fault?

_____

5. Look up <u>disrespected</u> in the dictionary. What does it mean, <u>in</u> <u>your</u> <u>own</u> <u>words</u>

_____

6. Why did he leave home? _____

_____

7. Why doesn't this man like the world? _____

_____

8. What does he mean when he says it's a "dog-eat-dog world"?

_____

_____

9. Why isn't it safe to walk the streets at night? _____

10. What do you think the man means by Cloud Nine? _____

_____

11. Do you think it is good that he is up on Cloud Nine all the time?

_____

12. Is it good for other people? Why? _____

_____

13. Choose two lines in the song that you like the best just because they sound good:

_____

_____

14. Would you want to be on Cloud Nine? Why? _____

_____

_____

October 28, 1971

GENERAL STATION

Name: _____

* Today let's learn how to use a simple code.

this is a way of making what you write secret. Only someone who
knows the code can de-code what you write and find out what
it says.

Write out the alphabet. Then write the alphabet backwards underneath. ⟵

A B C D E F G H I J K L M N O P Q R S T U V W X Y Z
Z Y X W V U T S R Q P O N M L K J I H G F E D C B A

In the code, each letter changes to the letter under it.

To de-code, do the same thing.
                                                            ↓

.* So — In code, D would be W   R would be ____
                 X would be ____   T would be ____
                 M would be ____   X would be ____

_____

* Now see if you can de-code these messages:

TVG GLTVGSVG — _____

GSV QZXPHLM UREV ZIV GSV TIVZ6UHG —

_____

GSV TLOW RH RM GSV XLUURM —

_____

* Now try making up some messages of your own. Get friends to de-code them.

_____
_____
_____

November 2, 1972   GENERAL STATION   Name: _____ ㉙

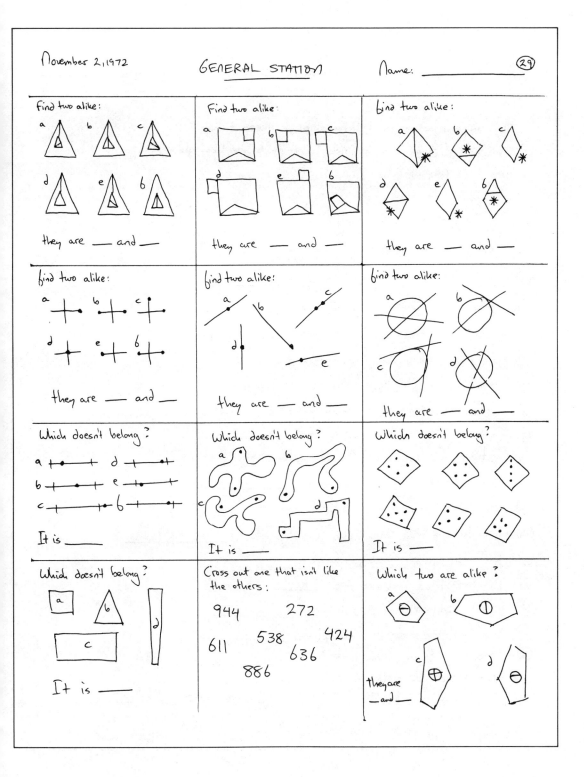

Find two alike:

a   b   c

d   e   b

they are __ and __

Find two alike:

a   b   c

d   e   b

they are __ and __

find two alike:

a   b   c

d   e   b

they are __ and __

find two alike:

a   b   c

d   e   b

they are __ and __

find two alike:

a   b   c

d   e

they are __ and __

find two alike:

a   b

c   d

they are __ and __

Which doesn't belong?

a   d

b   e

c   b

It is ____

Which doesn't belong?

a   b

c   d

It is ____

Which doesn't belong?

It is __

Which doesn't belong?

a   b

c   d

It is __

Cross out one that isn't like the others:

944   272

611   538   424
      636

886

Which two are alike?

a   b

c   d

they are __ and __

223

November 15, 1971   GENERAL STATION   Name: _____

This is a station on relationships between things.
This kind of thing is often used on tests to see how clever you are.
But they can also be fun.

① Father → son ,   mother → _____

② cat → mouse ,   tiger → _____

③ Spoon → soup ,   fork → _____

④ two → four ,   three → _____

⑤ leaf → tree ,   hair → _____

⑥ curtain → window,   clothes → _____

⑦ smoke → chimney ,   sewage → _____

⑧ clock → time ,   thermometer → _____

⑨ wheat → bread ,   poppies → _____

⑩ state → country ,   Massachusetts → _____

⑪ voice → song ,   legs → _____

⑫ man → impersonation ,   Flip Wilson → _____

⑬ Temptations → Cloud Nine ,   Sly → _____

⑭ bed → sleep ,   chair → _____

⑮ this → that,   here → _____

⑯ pencil → pen,   tricycle → _____

⑰ hospital → doctor ,   school → _____

⑱ love → kiss ,   hate → _____

CAN YOU MAKE UP ONE OF YOUR OWN ?

⑲ _____ → _____ , _____ → _____

November 15, 1971   <u>SPELLING STATION</u>   Name:_____

Put these ten new words into your dictionary.

Learn them as you write them in. We will work on them all week.

1. <u>chimney</u> - noun - a vertical shaft to carry away smoke from a fireplace
   The chimney was stopped up, so the smoke came into the room.

2. <u>echo</u> - noun - what you hear when a sound bounces off something and comes back to you
   He heard the echo of his voice down the long corridor.

3. <u>radar</u> - noun - a machine that can "see" things in the dark or the fog by bouncing
                      electromagnetic waves off them
   They could see the enemy planes coming on the radar screen.

4. <u>antidote</u> - noun - a medicine taken to cure you from a poison or a disease
   They gave her an antidote to the plague, and she didn't die of the disease.

5. <u>lawyer</u> - noun - a man or woman who knows all about laws and can argue in court
   The lawyer tried to save the man, but the judge found him guilty of murder.

6. <u>decoy</u> - noun - something to distract your attention from what you are really looking for
   All the tunnels on Oak Island might be a decoy; the treasure might be somewhere else.

7. <u>phony</u> - adjective - fake; not the real thing
   The man tried to give me some phony money, but I wouldn't take it.

8. <u>chronic</u> - adjective - lasts for a long time, lingers on
   For a whole week I had a chronic cough that wore out my throat.

9. <u>fluke</u> - noun - a lucky, accidental stroke
   He shot the basket from 50 feet away; by a fluke it went in.

10. <u>flunkey</u> - noun - your servant; someone who waits on you
    He treated his girlfriend like a flunkey; he made her do everything for him.

November 16, 1971   <u>SPELLING STATION</u>   Name:_____

Put yesterday's spelling words into the right slots:
chimney echo radar antidote lawyer decoy phony chronic fluke flunkey

Sentences

1. The man was arrested for trying to pass off a _____ ten-dollar bill.

2. They gave the girl the _____ for the plague just in time to save her life.

3. All he could hear was the _____ of his footsteps down the long corridor.

4. The boy filled out the test with his eyes closed, and by a _____ he got an A.

5. Some duck hunters use wooden ducks as _____s to get ducks to come close.

6. When the general saw the enemy planes coming on the _____ screen, he fainted.

7. If you treat your girlfriend like a _____, you won't have a girlfriend for long.

8. The lady had a _____ disease; after suffering for 17 years, she died.

9. Santa Claus is supposed to come down the _____, but we all know
   that he is too fat for that.

10. If you are ever arrested, you have the right to call a _____ to defend you.

Meanings

1. something to distract you attention from what you are really looking for - _____

2. a medicine taken to cure you from a poison or a disease - _____

3. a lucky, accidental shot - _____

4. fake - _____

5. a machine that can 'see' things in the dark or fog - _____

6. sound bouncing off something - _____

7. servant, someone who waits on you - _____

8. lasts for a long time - _____

9. a man or woman who knows a lot about laws and can argue in court - _____

10. a vertical shaft to carry away smoke from a fireplace or furnace - _____

November 17, 1971   SPELLING STATION   Name:_____

** Use each one of this week's spelling words in a good, long juicy sentence.
   If you aren't clear on the meaning, look it up in your Spelling Dictionary.

1. chimney _____

_____

2. echo _____

_____

3. radar _____

_____

4. antidote _____

_____

5. lawyer _____

_____

6. decoy _____

_____

7. phony _____

_____

8. chronic _____

_____

9. fluke _____

_____

10. flunkey _____

_____

SPELLING STATION

Name: _____

Find this week's and last week's spelling words in here. Good luck!
When you find them, write them below.

```
Y O C E D B D C L P Q R P T B G L R L P D M
P M L C M Z D T R Q D N H M E D Z A P R Q N
Q R O B A R E M T L S D O H A E R D W O I N
P D R Q P L D X C P N A N X R B E A R Y E L
N M D E T S A T Z H L Q Y U R Y S R T S E T
D F O P Y Z C M X W R C M Q L R C P Z V U R
M O L V E R D O Z M Q O R D E A F S T Q R P
Y M M U M M E C H O M M N D C S P L O Q L D
E Z Z N Z Z Z P P P R P I P S D L U M Z Q
N L N Y P K C D R Q M E D Z C E R Q L K D R
M G E M R Q E R Z D M F Q R D C L M Z M E A
I D H P A U D Y O H R F Q L L E D A H S T R
H L C M Q R T D M E T O D I T N A Z M Q S Z
C A T C M P L N Z M D Z R Q L Z R P L D A P
C D I M E C U D E W X M Z D A C E B C D T C
C D K P A M D E K C C E R W P I H S A M Q M
```

1 _____	11 _____	
2 _____	12 _____	
3 _____	13 _____	
4 _____	14 _____	
5 _____	15 _____	
6 _____	16 _____	
7 _____	17 _____	
8 _____	18 _____	
9 _____	19 _____	
10 _____	20 _____	

September 27, 1971   <u>ENGLISH STATION</u>   Name:_____

Today we are going to learn about the APOSTROPHE.
This is a little mark that looks like this '
Here are some places it goes: it's a nice day. It was Mike's book.

In fact there are two places it goes.

<u>THE FIRST</u> is at the end of a word with an s to make it possessive (to make something belong to it)

    Carol's watch   the school's gym   Lynn's folder   Kassedra's dress

Try turning these into possessive nouns:

1. the ball that belonged to John - ___John's ball_____

2. the shoe that belonged to Almaria - _____

3. the glasses that belonged to Mr. Marshall - _____

4. the purse that belonged to Lolethia - _____

5. the ring that belongs to Vickey - _____

        There's another thing to remember - with plural nouns (more than one)
        put the apostrophe at the very end - don't add another s.

6. the clothes that belonged to the girls - __the girls' clothes____

7. the basketball that belonged to the boys - _____

8. the licence plates that belonged to the cars - _____

9. the ribbons that belonged to the typewriters - _____

10. the room that belonged to the teachers - _____

<u>THE SECOND</u> place you use the apostrophe is for contractions.

    This is when you make two words shorter so they are quicker to say.
    The apostrophe takes the place of the letter you take out.

\ is not / \ do not / \ could not /
\ isn't /   \ don't /   \ couldn't /

See how many of these you can do:

have not - _____   there is - _____   he is - _____

does not - _____   she is - _____   are not - _____

was not - _____   will not - (careful!)_____   can not - _____

Today we are going to learn about synonyms, antonyms, and homonyms.

   Synonyms mean almost the same as each other.   Big and large are synonyms

   Antonyms mean the opposite.   Big and small are antonyms

   Homonyms just sound the same. Here and hear are homonyms

Tell which each of these are:

1. here and hear - _____   11. clean and dirty - _____

2. serious and happy - _____   12. nice and kind - _____

3. nice and good - _____   13. beach and beech - _____

4. hare and hair - _____   14. night and knight - _____

5. threw and through - _____   15. cool and chilly - _____

6. day and night - _____   16. boy and lad - _____

7. glad and happy - _____   17. hostile and friendly - _____

8. bear and bare - _____   18. city and metropolis - _____

9. blue and blew - _____   19. huge and enormous - _____

10. learning and education - _____   20. sight and site - _____

** Now.

1. Think of a homonym for seam - _____

2. Think of a synonym for lady - _____

3. Think of an antonym for cute - _____

4. Think of a synonym for damp - _____

5. Think of an antonym for fall - _____

6. Think of an antonym for lose - _____

** Now try making some pairs of your own:

SYNONYMS	ANTONYMS	HOMONYMS

The Story of November 3, 1971

November 3, 1971, which was yesterday, was a sorry day in the history of the King School. There were three fire alarms before recess, and on one of them we stayed out for a long time. In the afternoon there were more alarms. The seventh and eigth grade lunches were disturbed. No one got much work done, and several people were hurt during the alarms in fights and paper-clip shooting outside the school.

We all went home exhausted and tense. I talked with some friends in the school about what we could do, but none of us could think of any way. There was a teachers' meeting, and none of the teachers could think of a way that would stop the alarms. One teacher suggested that when teachers have a free period they should watch the boxes. But someone else pointed out that there aren't enough free periods for teachers to do this, and besides they need the time to do other things and rest from teaching.

For several weeks teachers have been talking about turning off all the fire alarms but the one by the office. But the firemen won't let us do this. They say that it would be dangerous if there was a real fire.

But some of the teachers say that the dangers of running in and out of the school, fighting, and having things shot at you are far greater than any fire in the school. They say that if there was a real fire, it wouldn't take long for someone to run down to the fire box by the office and ring that one. Then everyone would be safe, but we wouldn't have all the false alarms.

Another problem with the false alarms is that after a while the firemen don't take them seriously. When the bell rings down at the station, they say to one another, "Well, I guess that's another false one at the old King School." As a result, they don't get here as fast. If there was a real fire, this could be very dangerous.

So the teachers and Mrs. Brown, the Principal, have tried hard to get all the boxes but the one by the office turned off. But the firemen say they can't do it. They say there is a law that says there must be so many fire boxes they can't be turned off.

What the fire boxes do is give the power to ruin your education to a few mixed-up kids who are mad at someone or want to have fun. Maybe they don't know what they are doing to their brothers and sisters. Maybe they won't be there in a few years when you can't get into college or get a job because your education wasn't good enough. And maybe they just don't care.

So what are we going to do about it?

QUESTIONS AND OPINIONS:

1. How many alarms were there before recess yesterday?_____

2. How are kids hurt during alarms?

_____

_____

_____

3. Why can't the teachers mind the boxes?

_____

_____

4. If teachers could mind them, could they stop all the alarms?_____

How could kids ring them anyway?

_____

_____

_____

5. What is the other idea for stopping the false alarms?

_____

_____

6. What do you think of this idea and why?

_____

_____

_____

7. Why are the firemen against it?

_____

_____

8. What do you think should be done?

_____

_____

_____

_____

November 8, 1971   ENGLISH STATION   Name: _____

✳ Write as many words as you can think of for each vowel sound; at least fill the line

short ă (cat)	Long ā (sale)	short ě (bed)	long ē (be)	short ĭ (sit)	long ī (mile)
sat					
mat					

short ŏ (on)	long ō (note)	short ŭ (cup)	long ū (use)

✳ Tell whether these are short or long. Put ˘ over short vowels, ‾ over long ones.

tĕll   sēe   me   ask   but   cute   on   gun   those shop ice pick

gee   hope   equal   help   paper   black   ashes   imp   pie   hen   beg   he

✳ Draw lines between the words with the same vowel sound: ⟶

cute sun phone on mate at gee get mile big

buse gun me sit don moan pile sat gate met

This week we are going to learn all about how to put capitals. And where to put them.

** First of all, so we can be sure we know what is happening, write capitals for these:
   Write them in your most beautiful handwriting.

   a__ b__ c__ d__ e__ f__ g__ h__ i__ j__ k__ l__ m__ n__ o__ p__

   q__ r__ s__ t__ u__ v__ w__ x__ y__ z__

** Now read these ten rules for where to put capitals:

1. At the beginning of people's names.
2. At the beginning of the names of cities and places.
3. At the beginning of days of the week, months of the year, and holidays.
4. At the beginning of every sentence.
5. When you use the letter i by itself.
6. For races, nationalities, religions.
7. For words talking about God.
8. For all the big words in the titles of books, stories, movies, etc. (of, the, are little words)
9. At the beginning of a letter, when you write Dear ------,
10. The names of schools, companies, churches, and public buildings.

RULES

** Now write the whole rule by the place where it is used. Don't write the number only!!

1. King School - _____

2. November 15th - _____

3. Alphonso Anderson - _____

4. Dear President Nixon - _____

5. God and His son Jesus Christ - _____

6. ... she said I was nice - _____

7. she is Mexican - _____

8. we are in Roxbury - _____

9. a book called Soul on Ice - _____

10. They left yesterday - _____

11. it will be Christmas soon   _____

12. they saw the movie Shaft - _____

13. Kasanof's Bakery - _____

14. Negroes, Caucasians, and Orientals - _____

November 23, 1971   ENGLISH STATION   Name:_____

** Break these up into sentences (by putting periods and capitals):

1. She was fat and ugly most people didn't like her but she could play the
   piano beautifully (3 sentences)

2. i am cold i wish someone would heat this house properly i think I will go
   and take that landlord to court for not doing his job right (3 sentences)

3. angela Davis is being tried in California her trial has already lasted
   for a long time they are arguing about whether it should be held in
   another city angela Davis thinks the jury won't be fair in the city it
   is being held in now (4 sentences)

4. john Kennedy was killed in Dallas, Texas eight years ago yesterday he was
   a young and vigorous president he had a young beautiful wife he tried
   to do many things for America, but he didn't really get a chance to do
   much. (4 sentences)

5. i am sick i wish I felt better i got sick from the food at lunch i hope I'll
   feel better tomorrow (4 sentences)

** Now see how you do with this one:

     cynthia was late for school when she got there the front door was
locked she ran around to the kitchen door and knocked loudly after a
while one of the ladies opened the door and let her in when she got
to her class her teacher was very understanding and didn't keep her
after school

** Now write a paragraph of your own with at least five sentences.

234

November 30, 1971   READING STATION   Name:_____

The Black Police Patrol

There is a lot of crime in Roxbury. In fact
this neighborhood is the second worst place in
Boston for murders and hold-ups and muggings
and rapes (the South End is the worst). People
are afraid to walk the streets at night.

Recently the crime in Roxbury (and all over
America) has gotten a lot worse. The main
reason is the number of drug addicts there are
around these days. Drug addicts are the most
dangerous criminals in the world. Thay are
desperate to get money so they can buy more
heroin. They will do anything to get that money,
even if it means killing a person who has done
nothing to them.

In New York City, lots of people carry around
$100 with them all the time. If they get held
up by a heroin addict, they give the addict
the money right away. This is to make the addict
happy so he won't kill them. These people figure
that losing $100 is a lot better than losing
their life. And they are right. Lots of times
heroin addicts have killed people who didn't
have enough money because they were mad they
didn't have more or because they thought they
were hiding it somewhere.

Anyway, the crime in Roxbury has gotten a lot
worse since a lot of people got hooked on heroin.
The police don't seem to be able to catch the
pushers and the rich men in Cadillacs who bring
the heroin in. And they find it hard to stop
the number of murders and muggings and so on.
The police say it is because there aren't enough
policemen and because people in Roxbury won't
help them.

But lots of people in Roxbury, especially a
man named Jack Robinson (who is head of the
NAACP) think it is because the policemen are
white. They say that white policemen don't
know the community and the people. They say that
people don't trust the white policemen and so
they won't help them find criminals and drug
addicts.

In the last two weeks there have been three
murders in Roxbury. People decided that something
had to be done. So Mr. Robinson persuaded the
Boston Police Department to set up an all-black
police patrol. This patrol operates out of
Station 2 on the night shift, and is
made up of only black policemen. A lot of
people have complained about this. They say it
is discrimination, that you can't do things that
way. But the Police Department is going to try
it for a while and see if it cuts down on the
amount of crime in Roxbury. We will see what happens.

QUESTIONS:

1. What part of Boston has the most crime?

_____

2. Why are people afraid to walk the streets?

_____

_____

3. Why are drug addicts dangerous?

_____

_____

4. Why do people in NYC carry around $100?

_____

_____

_____

5. Why do the police say they can't stop
all the crime in Roxbury?

_____

_____

6. Why does Jack Robinson say they can't?

_____

_____

7. What do you think? Say why.

_____

_____

_____

8. What was the immediate reason why they
set up the all-black patrol?

_____

9. Why are some people against it?

_____

10. Do you think it will work? Say why.

_____

_____

235

October 12, 1971   MATH. STATION   Name: _____

Today we are going to learn how to add decimals and subtract decimals.
Now this may sound very hard, but there is only one thing that is
different from the kind of adding and subtracting you've been doing for years.

[REMEMBER] ⟶ * BRING THE DECIMAL STRAIGHT DOWN INTO THE ANSWER
        * *   ↓

TRY THESE:

```
    33.7          783.1         224.03         778.1
    21.8           93.2           1.92          29.1
 + 14.5         +  2.03        + 3.01         + 37.8
 ┌────·───┐     ┌──────────┐   ┌──────────┐   ┌──────────┐
 └────────┘     └──────────┘   └──────────┘   └──────────┘
```

Make sure the [decimal] is in the answer right
under the other ones!

───

Now do these. PLEASE don't make any silly mistakes in your adding and subtracting.

```
  228.14    (careful!)         774.1         994.21        692.47
+  77.91   subtraction 231.09   29.2        - 7.30         28.31
 ────────    ⟋  - 77.91       + 37.9        ───────       + 29.2
                ──────         ──────                      ──────
```

```
  778.94     69.1           69.241         789.12        695.003
-  3.25      22.1         -  7.014          29.14       - 12.931
 ───────     79.3          ───────          77.02        ───────
             29.4                           79.92
             77.9                           40.91
           + 44.1                           25.00
            ──────                        + 45.91
                                           ──────
```

[DID YOU REMEMBER ALL THE DECIMALS ??]

236

November 8, 1971

<u>MATH STATION</u>

Name: _____

* For each set of problems,
work out the times table
chart first. Then divide
and look back at the
chart to help you.

REMEMBER the
4 steps of long
division : ⟶

① divide
② multiply
③ subtract
④ bring down

21 × 1 = ___
  × 2 = ___
  × 3 = ___
  × 4 = ___
  × 5 = ___
  × 6 = ___
  × 7 = ___
  × 8 = ___
  × 9 = ___

21 ⟌ 798   21 ⟌ 525   21 ⟌ 1344

21 ⟌ 289 R. ___   21 ⟌ 443 R. ___

35 × 1 = ___
  × 2 = ___
  × 3 = ___
  × 4 = ___
  × 5 = ___
  × 6 = ___
  × 7 = ___
  × 8 = ___
  × 9 = ___

35 ⟌ 1575   35 ⟌ 2950

35 ⟌ 444 R. ___   35 ⟌ 9113 R. ___   35 ⟌ 1000 R. ___

January 7, 1971   MATH. STATION   Name: _____

There are 3 kinds of thing in geometry:
_1_ dimensional things : ⎯ ᜃ ᜃ ᜃ ᜃ
                          all of these are in _one_ dimension

_2_ dimensional things : ▭ ▢ ◯ ▱ ▱ ⌒ △
                          these are all _two_ dimensional - they are _closed_,
                          in other words the lines meet and close in
                          some space.

3 dimensional things :   ▭ ▭ ⬭ △ ◇
                          you can pick up these - they are _solid_.

※ Now write down whether these are 1, 2, or 3 - dimensional.
   Just write _1, 2, or 3_

(1) ⋀⋁ - _____   (8) ᜃ - _____   (15) ⬚ _____

(2) ▱ - _____   (9) ⊔ - _____   (16) ⌇ _____

(3) ╱ - _____   (10) ⬤ _____   (17) ⬠ _____

(4) ᒣᒣ - _____   (11) ▭ _____   (18) • _____

(5) △ - _____   (12) △ _____   (19) ◈ _____

(6) ⋀ - _____   (13) ☁ _____   (20) 🍾 _____

(7) ▭ - _____   (14) ⌐ _____

May 3, 1971

Name:_____

$\frac{1}{8}$ $\frac{3}{5}$ $\frac{7}{8}$ $\frac{9}{10}$ $\frac{6}{7}$ $\frac{9}{13}$ $\frac{1}{2}$ $\frac{2}{3}$ $\frac{7}{9}$ $\frac{4}{5}$ $\frac{2}{5}$ $\frac{7}{10}$ $\frac{10}{11}$ $\frac{2}{5}$ $\frac{9}{82}$ $\frac{2}{7}$

Today we are going to start fractions, which we will do for the rest of the year.

First of all, what is a fraction?

A FRACTION IS A PART OF SOMETHING.

- like half an apple pie → $\frac{1}{2}$
- a quarter of a dollar → $\frac{1}{4}$
- half an hour → $\frac{1}{2}$

LEARN → THIS [The top of every fraction is called the numerator. This tells how many pieces there are. The bottom of all fractions is called the denominator. This tells how many pieces the whole thing is cut up into.

ANSWER THESE QUESTIONS FROM THIS :

1. What is a fraction? _____

2. Give five examples of a fraction: 1. _____

   2. _____

   3. _____

   4. _____

   5. _____

3. In this fraction, $\frac{1}{4}$, what is the 1 called? _____

   what is the 4 called? _____

4. In this fraction, $\frac{1}{2}$, how many pieces are there? _____

   How many pieces is the thing cut up into? _____

NOW WRITE WHAT THE SHADED PART IS CALLED AS A FRACTION:

how much shaded? 1 how many pieces? 3	is ___	is ___	is ___	is ___
is ___	is ___	is ___	is ___	is ___